Brokenness to Beauty
Bible Study

Going Deeper to the Source of Transforming
Your Brokenness to Beauty

Jacqueline Wallace

WESTBOW
PRESS®
A DIVISION OF THOMAS NELSON
& ZONDERVAN

Contents

Acknowledgements

Once again, I am indebted to many people for the assistance given to me as I wrote this Bible study. I knew from my experience writing the book, *Brokenness to Beauty: Transforming Your Brokenness into a Beautiful Life,* how valuable it was to have a small group of women, a beta group, to work through each lesson with me as I wrote it. It is always good to have more eyes looking at what you've written, so you can see it better yourself.

We still lived in Bakersfield, CA, when I started writing the Bible study lessons. We'd been active members in the church for over three years at that point so I knew a number of women. I invited Naomi Chow, Morgan Gerlings, Sam Hulse, and Karri Rogge to join me in this venture of working through each lesson as I wrote it. We met once a week, those weeks stretching into several months. We got through all but the final one, Lesson 10, before I moved to southern California.

I also called on members of my writer's critique group once again. Mikie Pyle, Sharon Miller, Donna Hudson, and Bethane Banks emailed me their critiques.

After our move "down south" from Bakersfield to southern California, I had to form another beta group of women who would be willing to meet weekly and critique the final lesson of the Bible study. In the end, I gained the commitment of four ladies from my new church: Angie Wood, Titi Akenremi, Dena Leavitt, and Verenna McLeod. Not only did they work through Lesson 10 of the study with me, but they wanted to go back and work through all nine of the previous lessons since they hadn't had that opportunity previously. So we did just that.

Another friend who critiqued my writing is Steve Holloway. My husband and I have known Steve and his wife, Kitty, since the 1980s. When I learned Steve was writing his first novel, inviting others to critique his work, I volunteered for a time. Fascinating story! I look forward to the finished product. I invited him to critique my Bible study and he gave valuable insight and posed questions and suggested articles and books I'd never considered before.

All these friends' insights and suggestions helped make this Bible study better and I heartily thank each one.

Of course, the most faithful supporter and friend in all my endeavors, whether writing a book or Bible study, starting a mission group at church, or needing extra help at home because of a health downturn, is my husband, Randy. Thank you for loving me, believing in me, and encouraging me to do all God puts on my heart. And thank you for first and foremost loving our Lord and God who has given us all these good people and all good things in our lives.

I thank God for the opportunity to do this writing. My prayer is that it will benefit others on their journey through life.

Introduction

Why does anyone write a Bible study? I'm sure there are as many reasons as there are Bible studies on the market.

When my sister-in-law, Michele (who wrote the Foreword to *Brokenness to Beauty*), and I were first talking about me writing a book, we discussed the idea of including a Bible study component. Sounded like a good idea. Daunting and intimidating too!

I had started writing *Brokenness to Beauty* with the Bible study component in the back of my mind. But so much water poured over the dam of my life, so to speak, in the years it took me to write that book, by the time I neared publication that's all I wanted to do—get it published!

So why did I write a Bible study companion to *Brokenness to Beauty*? Here's why. When women read my book, *Brokenness to Beauty*, they often asked me if I'd written a Bible study to go with it. Time after time, I heard that question. Some women made up their own study questions to go with the chapters and worked through them in their Bible study groups.

Okay, I thought. Something is going on here. I became convinced I should write a Bible study based on what I wanted to point out and expand upon from the various truths touched on in those chapters. My desire is always to point people back to the Scriptures to discover "What saith the Lord?" What he says is the only thing that really matters.

That is why I wrote this Bible study companion to *Brokenness to Beauty*, to hear from God himself, through his written word, more of what he has to say about issues raised in the book, *Brokenness to Beauty*.

Writing a Bible study is much different from writing a book. *Brokenness to Beauty* has twenty-three chapters. Not many people will go through a Bible study of twenty-three lessons, especially for group studies. Instead, I had to combine two to four chapters of the book into one lesson for several of the Bible study lessons. I came up with ten lessons from those twenty-three book chapters. There is leeway to stretch or condense them into more or less than ten lessons, as desired.

You will see that a pattern of Read, Respond, and Resolve repeats in each lesson. First, there is required Reading before and during the lesson. You will also memorize a verse for the week.

Then you are asked to Respond by thinking through and answering a series of questions based on at least one topic from the selected reading from the book's chapters and the Scriptures.

Finally, at the end of each lesson, you will Resolve (promise) to follow through with actions based on what the Scriptures taught through that lesson. Those promises are commitments you make to yourself and God and are there because simply reading what God says is not enough; we must put his words into practice.

The lessons are also broken into sections as numbered days: Day 1, Day 2, and so on. This is for your convenience but is optional. Move through the lessons at your own speed. Make the lessons work for you.

Lesson 1 is all about telling your story. That's what I did in the first chapter of my book. Everyone has a story and we can learn how to look at our lives in such a way to give glory to God as we tell others about what he has done in us. Telling our story to glorify God is more significant than we realize.

In Lesson 2 we look at the only Foundation worth building our lives on, and follow up in Lesson 3 with the how and why of building well on that foundation.

Do you sense your need of hope in life's struggles? If there is one thing we all need today it is hope. Lesson 4 pulls us into the Scriptures to show us where and how to find hope in our everyday struggles.

Lesson 5 considers, from God's Word, how to hear him well, trust him fully, see God for who he is, and learn to view life from his perspective. Mastering these skills makes a world of difference in navigating both the good and bad days of our lives.

Lesson 6 moves into the realm of prayer where we look into the Word of God to learn what he has to say about how he wants us to relate to him, and what our spirit has to do with prayer. Finally, we look at the significance of our words. Are our words important to God?

Lesson 7 takes a closer look at faith as it relates to prayer. What is this thing called faith and why is it important in prayer?

In Lesson 8 we discover from many Scriptures the truth that calls us to be persistent in prayer. It's all there for us to mine out, if we have the will to do it.

Lesson 9 of the Bible study combines all four chapters of Part 4, "Community," of the book, *Brokenness to Beauty*. We will look into many passages of Scripture that beautifully portray Christian community and learn from them what Christian community is and how it operates. We need one another and no more so than when we are suffering. Others need us, too, and we can see how believers in the past "gave back" in gratitude and love to their community of support.

The final lesson of the study is Lesson 10. What gets you up and going on your most difficult days? A strong cup of coffee? Wee ones climbing into bed with you, signaling the end of taking it easy for that day? There is something much greater, much more motivating and lasting. Even coffee and clamoring children lose their power with the changing circumstances of life; our physical needs change and children grow up. Lesson 10 will prod and call you to rise up to meet that greater challenge, the challenge that will never change.

After Lesson 10 you will find a Growth Through Crisis Worksheet. Crises in our lives can be times of deep spiritual growth. If you are currently in or have gone through a time of crisis, use this worksheet as a tool to assist in cooperating with God as he works to develop the character of Christ in you through the difficult times of life.

Words to Live By
Bible Study Group Etiquette

"This is my commandment: love each other just as I have loved you.
No one has greater love than to give up one's life for one's friends."
~ Jesus (John 15:12–13 CEB)

This is Jesus' last command to his followers before his death. He emphasized agape love as he talked with them on their last evening together, and demonstrated it by washing their feet at their last meal. Then he showed them that "greater love," the ultimate expression of love, when he submitted to crucifixion and death for them and for us all.

Although most of us don't like to be told what to do, Jesus' command to love one another falls on us now. And we must be very clear that it is a command, not a suggestion. We can show love for one another in a multitude of ways, from very easy to extremely risky. For your time together in this Bible study, you have the opportunity (and responsibility) to love one another in some rather easy ways by carrying out these simple guidelines. Value each person in your little community of the Bible study group. Give to one and all the respect due them. Commit to:

1. Show up. Someone said that 90% of any task is just showing up. Be at the group meetings (barring an emergency). And when there, be present. "Be Here Now," attentive and engaged in the moment. This is for your own benefit as well as the benefit of the others. You never know what God may speak to you through another person, or what God may impress on another through you. Sometimes you just being there is all the encouragement someone else needs (Hebrews 10:24–25).

2. Do your work. The week before you meet, do the work for the upcoming lesson in preparation for the group time. The more effort you put into the study, the more you will get out of it. Solomon said, "The soul (appetite) of the lazy person craves and gets nothing [for lethargy overcomes ambition], but the soul (appetite)

of the diligent [who works willingly] is rich and abundantly supplied" (Proverbs 13:4 AMP).

3. Be generous and share the discussion time. Be short-winded so others may also participate in the discussions (1 Peter 5:5–7).

4. Be quicker to listen than to give advice. Bible study discussions are not the place for advising or counseling. You are not meeting together to solve anyone's problems but to listen and learn what God has to say in his Word. "Understand this, my beloved brothers and sisters. Let everyone be quick to hear [be a careful, thoughtful listener], slow to speak [a speaker of carefully chosen words and], slow to anger [patient, reflective, forgiving] (James 1:19 AMP).

5. Be trustworthy as you listen. Personal issues shared in the group discussions stay a secret with the group. These things are not to be told to anyone else. "He who goes about as a gossip reveals secrets, but he who is trustworthy and faithful keeps a matter hidden" (Proverbs 11:13 AMP).

6. Be a Berean Christian. When questions come up, don't default to traditional, current, or even "common sense" ideas, but search the Scriptures like the Bereans did to find out what God has to say about the issue. He does have a word to say about it. And unlike the words of men, God's Word endures forever (Acts 17:10–12; 1 Thessalonians 5:21; 1 Peter 1:22–25).

These are easy, yet thoughtful ways we can love one another in any group setting and these few guidelines will serve as our standard of etiquette for this Bible study group.

Enjoy your time together!

Bible Study Methods

This Bible study uses several simple methods or techniques to help you, the student, get a better understanding of what the verses and passages of the Bible actually say. Below is a closer look at the techniques used so that you can carry them over into your personal, ongoing times of study of the Bible.

1. Read and re-read the verse or passage of Scripture throughout the week. This is probably the most important technique for getting a good grasp of the Scriptures as you study.

2. Memorize Scripture. The value of this discipline cannot be over-estimated. When we get the Word into our minds, it can get down into our hearts and the Spirit can bring it out to:

   a. Recall it to mind as we read other passages of Scripture. Comparing Scripture with Scripture gives us enlightenment and understanding of the Word. "The unfolding of Your words gives light, it gives understanding …" (Psalm 119:130).
   b. Guide our decisions. "Your word is a lamp to my feet and a light to my path" (Psalm 119:105).
   c. Keep us from sin. "Your word have I treasured in my heart, that I may not sin against You" (Psalm 119:11).
   d. Enable us to use pertinent Scripture at crucial points in conversation. "Like apples of gold in settings of silver is a word spoken in right circumstances" (Proverbs 25:11).

3. Use more than one reliable Bible translation or version to get a fuller grasp of the meaning of the verse or passage of Scripture.

4. Circle, underline, or highlight repeated words or phrases, or groups of similar words such as nouns, verbs, or adjectives. This helps us categorize valuable information about the subject(s) of our study, such as learning what God is like or what we humans are like (attributes and characteristics).

5. Note the direct commands; these are our "To Do's" in Scripture.

6. Write out the commands found in the verses, what our responses to them should be, and why we should respond that way (I Should/So That).

7. Write down contrasts, such as Philippians 3: 7–14, contrasting these with verses 18–19 of the same chapter.

8. Write down what you learned from the Scripture when you circled or underlined words or phrases. Listing these words is a simple way of seeing what is in the verse or passage.

9. List cause and effect such as, "Since God Is/Does," "I Will/Can." This practice solidifies what your desired response should be to that Scripture.

10. Group together verses or sections of Scripture that deal with a similar topic. See Lesson 2 for an example (Who Is Jesus Christ?).

11. Use a concordance to look up a word you recall from a verse to aid in locating that verse in the Bible. It is best to use a concordance that is in the same version as the Bible you are using so that the same words used in that translation of the Scripture can be found in the concordance (e.g. King James or NIV, etc.).

12. Use study tools like Mounce's *Interlinear for the Rest of Us*. This reverse Interlinear English /Greek testament shows the original Greek or Aramaic words used in the New Testament and their meanings.

13. Personalize the Psalms as you read them. Make the psalmist's prayers your own.

14. Pray the prayers in the Bible. As you read Scripture, highlight whole prayers you come across and incorporate these into your prayers.

If all this seems daunting, start with one thing, and at your own pace add other methods to your routine. The point of all this is to enhance your times in the Word with our Lord so you can rightly put the Word into practice. God's Spirit is our teacher and we, like all students, must listen and learn well, using the best tools and methods of study at our disposal.

It takes effort and diligence to be a good student of the Scriptures, but it is well worth the time and effort because by our study we can come to know *about* him, and by the transforming power of God's Word come to *really know* him and live a life worthy of him, pleasing our heavenly Father. "Be diligent to present yourself approved to God as a workman who does not need to be ashamed, accurately handling the word of truth" (2 Timothy 2:15).

"Therefore we also have as our ambition … to be pleasing to him" (2Corinthians 5:9).

We can make God smile.

Lesson 1

The Power of Story

Day 1
Everyone Has a Story

Read: *Brokenness to Beauty,* Part 1—My Story

Chapter 1, "Then to Now"
Read Psalm 145 every day during the week you study. Choose at least one verse and memorize it.

> It is out of these experiences I write. ... My life path is not one I would
> have chosen, but since it has been my life and I have learned much
> as I've lived it, I want to share ... what God has been teaching me.
> (*Brokenness to Beauty,* 11)

Respond:

Everyone has a story. *You* have a story.
1. Think back through your life. Write a short overview of it, starting with your childhood and moving on to today, hitting the lows, the highs, and the significant events as you recall them. Read it aloud to yourself. This is only for your eyes and ears. (You may want to write on a separate sheet.)

_____

_____

_____

2. Now, turn this page sideways, draw a horizontal line through the center of the page, and make a timeline of your life, marking the high and low points on it.

Day 2

Pass It On

Amy Carmichael, quoted in the final paragraph of chapter 1 of *Brokenness to Beauty*, believed we should share with others the things God teaches us, because the lessons are not just for ourselves alone.

1. Read Psalm 145:4. What does this verse affirm in light of Amy Carmichael's statement?

    _____

2. Read all of Psalm 145 (NIV), quoted here:

> I will exalt you, my God the King;
> I will praise your name for ever and ever.
> [2] Every day I will praise you
>   and extol your name for ever and ever.
> [3] Great is the Lord and most worthy of praise;
>   his greatness no one can fathom.
> [4] One generation commends your works to another;
>   they tell of your mighty acts.
> [5] They speak of the glorious splendor of your majesty—
>   and I will meditate on your wonderful works.
> [6] They tell of the power of your awesome works—
>   and I will proclaim your great deeds.
> [7] They celebrate your abundant goodness
>   and joyfully sing of your righteousness.
> [8] The Lord is gracious and compassionate,
>   slow to anger and rich in love.
> [9] The Lord is good to all;
>   he has compassion on all he has made.
> [10] All your works praise you, Lord;
>   your faithful people extol you.
> [11] They tell of the glory of your kingdom
>   and speak of your might,
> [12] so that all people may know of your mighty acts
>   and the glorious splendor of your kingdom.

¹³ Your kingdom is an everlasting kingdom,
   and your dominion endures through all generations.
The Lord is trustworthy in all he promises
   and faithful in all he does.
¹⁴ The Lord upholds all who fall
   and lifts up all who are bowed down.
¹⁵ The eyes of all look to you,
   and you give them their food at the proper time.
¹⁶ You open your hand
   and satisfy the desires of every living thing.
¹⁷ The Lord is righteous in all his ways
   and faithful in all he does.
¹⁸ The Lord is near to all who call on him,
   to all who call on him in truth.
¹⁹ He fulfills the desires of those who fear him;
   he hears their cry and saves them.
²⁰ The Lord watches over all who love him,
   but all the wicked he will destroy.
²¹ My mouth will speak in praise of the Lord.
   Let every creature praise his holy name
   for ever and ever.

a. First, circle every word or phrase in the psalm that is an adjective (descriptive word), attribute (character trait), or action ascribed to the Lord.
    Examples:
    v. 3: "Great [descriptive word] is the LORD and most worthy of praise [descriptive phrase]."
    v. 19: "He fulfills the desires [action word] of those who fear Him."

b. Next, underline every action made by the psalmist or others.
    Examples:
    v. 1: "I will exalt you, my God the King."
    v. 15: "The eyes of all look to you."

c. Under the appropriate headings below, list the circled or underlined phrases from Psalm 145.

The Lord Is/Does	I/We Will
_____	_____
_____	_____
_____	_____
_____	_____
_____	_____
_____	_____
_____	_____
_____	_____
_____	_____
_____	_____

d. Look again at the list you made of God's actions and attributes (left-hand column) from Psalm 145. What did you learn about God? (Pay close attention to verses 8–20.)

_____

_____

_____

e. Review the list in the right-hand column from Psalm 145, "I/We Will." What did you learn about how you and others should respond to who God is and what he has done?

_____

_____

3. In what way does the knowledge of God gleaned from Psalm 145 change your view of him in relation to your present circumstances or recent trials? For example, do you believe, as the psalmist says, that:

a. he cares for you,
b. he is trustworthy and faithful,
c. hc is sovereign over all people and events,
d. he always does what is right, and
e. he hears your cries.

4. Don't simply say yes or no to the examples above. Write what you believe is true about God based on the psalm you read. (Refer back to the two lists you made.)

Since God is _____, I can _____.

Since God is _____, I can _____.

Since God is _____, I can _____.

Since God can/does _____, I will _____.

Since God can/does _____, I will _____.

Since God can/does _____, I will _____.

Day 3
Saying "I Will"

1. Now, re-read Psalm 145 and personalize it by making the "I" of the psalmist yourself, as though you wrote the psalm. Substitute your troubles and fears for David's troubles and fears. Embrace the words of Scripture and speak them from your heart.

   Living by faith means that we believe the words about God in the Bible—who he is and what he is like—and then we act on that belief. We do not simply "have faith in faith." Our faith should be rooted in the personal God who has revealed himself in the Bible, not in our ideas about him.

   a. In light of your present circumstances and struggles, regardless of your emotions, will you choose to acknowledge God for who he is and slip into his embrace so you can experience his mighty acts of compassion and grace?

   _____

   b. What decisions have you made as to how you will live because of learning the words of truth about God and yourself in this psalm? Do your decisions line up with the "I will" of Psalm 145? Take time to write them here before moving on to the next question.

   _____

   _____

   _____

   _____

Day 4

Giving It Up

1. Revisit your life-story timeline. Can you see the mercies and kindnesses of God toward you? Pinpoint the times you recognize his interventions in your life. These "mighty acts" may not be big or flashy; some might be quiet and deeply personal. Write these into your timeline.

   Perhaps, as you reviewed your life story, things came to mind that you have done that you are not proud of, or things that were done to you for which you carry a load of guilt and shame. Or maybe you feel you have achieved great strides by your own efforts. You may have a mix of shame, guilt, and pride.

   I challenge you to listen closely and meditate on what Paul the apostle said. He was a super-Pharisee climbing to the top of his profession, and then he became a rabid persecutor of the church. But he ultimately became one of the most passionate followers of Jesus Christ who ever lived.

   > For we ... put no confidence in the flesh, although I myself might have confidence even in the flesh. If anyone else had a mind to put confidence in the flesh, I far more. ... But whatever things were gain to me, those things I have counted as loss for the sake of Christ. More than that, I count all things to be loss in view of the surpassing value of knowing Christ Jesus my Lord, for whom I have suffered the loss of all things, and count them but rubbish so that I may gain Christ, and may be found in Him, not having a righteousness of my own derived from the Law, but that which is through faith in Christ, the righteousness which comes from God on the basis of faith, that I may know Him and the power of His resurrection and the fellowship of His sufferings, being conformed to His death; in order that I may attain to the resurrection from the dead.
   > Not that I have already obtained it or have already become perfect, *but I press on so that I may lay hold of that for which also I was laid hold of by Christ Jesus.*
   > Brethren, I do not regard myself as having laid hold of it yet; but *one thing I do: forgetting what lies behind and reaching forward to what lies ahead, I press on* toward the goal for the prize of the upward call of God in Christ Jesus.
   > Let us therefore, as many as are perfect [mature], have this attitude; and if in anything you have a different attitude, God will reveal that

also to you; however, let us keep living by that same standard to which we have attained.

Brethren, join in following my example, and observe those who walk according to the pattern you have in us. (Philippians 3:3–17, emphasis added)

Spend some time re-reading and thinking your way through that passage. Grasp ahold of its meaning.

New Beginning

1. What do you need to let go of and count as loss and rubbish—both the good and the bad—for the sake of knowing Jesus Christ more deeply and accomplishing that for which God redeemed you?

_____

_____

_____

2. Will you embrace the attitude of Paul, forgetting what is behind and pressing ahead for God's glory? Will you use your own story to tell the good news of God and his works?

_____

Day 5
Go and Tell

1. Read again Psalm 145:4.

   a. What do you think the phrase "one generation shall praise your works to another" means?

   _____

   b. Who might some of those people be in "another" generation?

   _____

   _____

We tell others about God's mighty work through Jesus Christ—his death, resurrection, and ascension to heaven—to forgive us of our sins and give us new life in Christ. We tell them how we recognize him at work in our lives.

These people can include those who are older than we are, those who are younger, and those in our own age group; parents, children, grandchildren, extended family members, spouses; church family, coworkers, classmates, neighbors, community members; people you see frequently around town in stores and other establishments. You influence all of these people by your life, to some degree. They are the generations you speak to, proclaiming the mighty acts of God—his goodness and graciousness to you—for his glory and praise. If we do not tell it to them, how will they know the truth of this God we love and serve?

What is one thing you learned from this lesson?

_____

What are you going to do about it?

_____

_____

Resolve to:

1. Rearrange my life to be in the Word of God regularly, ideally every day (Deuteronomy 6:6–9; 17:14, 18–20; 29:29; and 32:46–47; Joshua 1:8; Matthew 7:24–27; Romans 12:2). How will you do that?

_____

2. Personalize and embrace God's words as I read Scripture (Psalm 1; Matthew 7:24–27; 2 Timothy 2:15; 3:14–17; James 1:22–25).

3. Look for ways to share with others a part of my life story where I recognize that God was at work. Use my story to point to the graciousness of God—and give him praise—for demonstrating his kindness, love, patience, and forgiveness to me. Share how God has changed me through his redemptive work in my life (Deuteronomy 6:6–7; 29:29; 32:46, 47; Psalm 22:28, 30–31; Psalm 63:1–8; Psalm 78:4–7; 79:13; Galatians 1:11–14).

4. Cultivate a lifestyle of recognizing God at work in and around me, making praise my default response to whatever happens in my life (Psalm 63: 1–8; Hebrews 13:12–16).

_____ (Initial here)

"Go home to your people and report to them what great things
the Lord has done for you, and how He had mercy on you."
(Mark 5:19)

Lesson 2

Following the Rock Called Jesus

Day 1
One Foundation ...

Read: *Brokenness to Beauty,* Part 2—The Bible

Chapter 3, "Foundations"
Read Colossians 1:9–23 every day this week. Choose at least one verse and memorize it.

> The Scriptures nurtured me daily, calling me back to the foundation of my life, giving me not only encouragement and hope but perspective. They acted like a compass, guiding me through the wind and waves of the storm in which I found myself. ... the compass of God's Word enabled me to move in the right direction, in hope and trust in the Lord. (*Brokenness to Beauty,* 23)

Respond:

1. Circle the sentence below that best describes your understanding of the importance of the Bible in your life.

   I know the Bible has affected my life in positive ways.
   I think the Bible has been good for me but I cannot specifically say how.
   I've heard that reading the Bible is important and I want to learn more.

I don't know anything about the Bible or why it should be important to me.
I've read parts of the Bible and had a negative experience with Christianity.

2. Explain why you chose your answer.

    _____

    _____

3. Read 1 Corinthians 3:10–17.

    a. Paul clearly states that there is only one foundation of the church, and for
        our lives as believers. What is that foundation? (v. 11)

        _____

    b. What do you think Paul means when he says Jesus Christ is the only
        foundation that can be laid?

        _____

    c. Look up the following Scriptures and record what each says about Jesus
        Christ.
        Matthew 16:15–17 _____

        Luke 24:25–27 ("Moses" refers to the first five books of the Jewish Scriptures,
        the Old Testament of the Christian Bible; "the Prophets" refers to many of the
        other books of the Old Testament.)

        _____

        Acts 2:22–36; 4:8–12

        _____

        _____

        _____

        _____

        Ephesians 2:19–22 _____
        1 Peter 2:2–6 _____
        Acts 4:10–12 _____

    d. What part of the foundation is Jesus?

        _____

From these Bible passages (and there are many others), we can see the roles that
are played by

- the prophecies of the Word of God (Luke 24:25–27, 1 Peter 2:2),
- the preaching and teaching of the Word (Acts 2:22–36; 4:8-12, Ephesians 2:19–22),
- and the work of the Spirit of God (Matthew 16:17; Acts2:22)

in laying the foundation of Jesus Christ for eternal salvation. Jesus Christ and his finished work on Calvary comprise the foundation of our faith, our salvation, and our relationship with God. He is the only foundation of the church, of which every believer is a part. This is what Paul means by Jesus Christ being the only foundation that can be laid for salvation.

Day 2
Who is this Jesus?

Let's pause a moment and ask this fundamental question:
Who is Jesus Christ? Why should we listen to him and do what he says?
As you read through each set of the verses below, write in the margin of the page short descriptions of what you learn about *who Jesus is* and/or *what he has done* or *will do*. It may be helpful to read one or two other Bible translations or versions as well, to get a clearer understanding of the passage.

Hebrews 1:1–3
"God, after He spoke long ago to the fathers in the prophets in many portions and in many ways, in these last days has spoken to us in His Son, whom He appointed heir of all things, through whom also He made the world. And He is the radiance of His glory and the exact representation of His nature, and upholds all things by the word of His power. When He had made purification of sins, He sat down at the right hand of the Majesty on high."

John 1:1–3, 11–14, 17
"In the beginning was the Word, and the Word was with God, and the Word was God. He was in the beginning with God. All things came into being through Him, and apart from Him nothing came into being that has come into being.
"He came to His own, and those who were His own did not receive Him. But as many as received Him, to them He gave the right to become children of God, even to those who believe in His name, who were born, not of blood nor of the will of the flesh nor of the will of man, but of God.
"And the Word became flesh, and dwelt among us, and we saw His glory, glory as of the only begotten from the Father, full of grace and truth. ... For the Law was given through Moses; grace and truth were realized through Jesus Christ."

Colossians 1:15–20

"He is the image of the invisible God, the firstborn of all creation. For by Him all things were created, both in the heavens and on earth, visible and invisible, whether thrones or dominions or rulers or authorities—all things have been created through Him and for Him. He is before all things, and in Him all things hold together. He is also head of the body, the church; and He is the beginning, the firstborn from the dead, so that He Himself will come to have first place in everything. For it was the Father's good pleasure for all the fullness to dwell in Him, and through Him to reconcile all things to Himself, having made peace through the blood of His cross; through Him, I say, whether things on earth or things in heaven."

John 3:16–18

"For God so loved the world, that He gave His only begotten Son, that whoever believes in Him shall not perish, but have eternal life. For God did not send the Son into the world to judge the world, but that the world might be saved through Him. He who believes in Him is not judged; he who does not believe has been judged already, because he has not believed in the name of the only begotten Son of God."

1 Corinthians 15:3–4

"For I delivered to you as of first importance what I also received, that Christ died for our sins according to the Scriptures, and that He was buried, and that He was raised on the third day according to the Scriptures."

Acts 4:12

"There is salvation in no one else; for there is no other name under heaven that has been given among men by which we must be saved."

God mercifully made a way of salvation because we "all have sinned and fall short of the glory of God" (Romans 3:23) and "the wages of sin is death, but the free gift of God is eternal life in Christ Jesus our Lord" (Romans 6:23). "This is eternal life, that they may know You, the only true God, and Jesus Christ whom You have sent" (John 17:3).

He has not left us alone in the world but has sent his Spirit to be with us. He lives in those who believe, so that we can carry on his work in the world until he returns to set up his kingdom.

John 14:16–17

"I will ask the Father, and He will give you another Helper, that He may be with you forever; that is the Spirit of truth, whom the world cannot receive, because it does not see Him or know Him, but you know Him because He abides with you and will be in you."

Acts 1:8–11
"You will receive power when the Holy Spirit has come upon you; and you shall be My witnesses both in Jerusalem, and in all Judea and Samaria, and even to the remotest part of the earth.

"And after He had said these things, He was lifted up while they were looking on, and a cloud received Him out of their sight. And as they were gazing intently into the sky while He was going, behold, two men in white clothing stood beside them. They also said, 'Men of Galilee, why do you stand looking into the sky? This Jesus, who has been taken up from you into heaven, will come in just the same way as you have watched Him go into heaven.'"

1 Thessalonians 4:16–17
"The Lord Himself will descend from heaven with a shout, with the voice of the archangel and with the trumpet of God, and the dead in Christ will rise first. Then we who are alive and remain will be caught up together with them in the clouds to meet the Lord in the air, and so we shall always be with the Lord."

Revelation 1:1–2, 9–10, 12–18
"The Revelation of Jesus Christ, which God gave Him to show to His bond-servants, the things which must soon take place; and He sent and communicated it by His angel to His bond-servant John, who testified to the word of God and to the testimony of Jesus Christ, even to all that he saw.

"I, John, your brother and fellow partaker in the tribulation and kingdom and perseverance which are in Jesus ... heard behind me a loud voice like the sound of a trumpet. ... Then I turned to see the voice that was speaking with me. ...

"I saw one like a son of man, clothed in a robe reaching to the feet, and girded across His chest with a golden sash. His head and His hair were white like white wool, like snow; and His eyes were like a flame of fire. His feet were like burnished bronze, when it has been made to glow in a furnace, and His voice was like the sound of many waters. In His right hand He held seven stars, and out of His mouth came a sharp two-edged sword; and His face was like the sun shining in its strength.

"When I saw Him, I fell at His feet like a dead man. And He placed His right hand on me, saying, 'Do not be afraid; I am the first and the last, and the living One; and I was dead, and behold, I am alive forevermore, and I have the keys of death and of Hades.'"

Revelation 5:11–12

"Then I looked, and I heard the voice of many angels around the throne and the living creatures and the elders; and the number of them was myriads of myriads, and thousands of thousands, saying with a loud voice,

'Worthy is the Lamb that was slain to receive power and riches and wisdom and might and honor and glory and blessing.'"

Revelation 21:1–4

"Then I saw a new heaven and a new earth; for the first heaven and the first earth passed away, and there is no longer any sea. And I saw the holy city, new Jerusalem, coming down out of heaven from God, made ready as a bride adorned for her husband. And I heard a loud voice from the throne, saying, 'Behold, the tabernacle of God is among men, and He will dwell among them, and they shall be His people, and God Himself will be among them, and He will wipe away every tear from their eyes; and there will no longer be any death; there will no longer be any mourning, or crying, or pain; the first things have passed away.'"

Revelation 22:7

"Behold, I am coming quickly. Blessed is he who heeds the words of the prophecy of this book."

This is who Jesus Christ is! This is why we listen to him and do what he says. He is God the Son. He is our Savior. The Old Testament is filled with prophesies about him and he fulfilled them all. In him alone is salvation and he alone is the foundation of the church. He is Lord. He is worthy. And he is the soon-coming King who will rule forever and ever!

... Many Builders

1. Read 1 Corinthians 3:11–17; 1 Peter 4–5.
   There is but one true foundation of the church and of our individual lives as believers: Jesus Christ. But there are many who build on that foundation: teachers, preachers, and ourselves. All have a responsibility to build with the right materials.

2. Read Matthew 7:24–27, Romans 12:1–2, James 1:21–25, and 1 Peter 1:22; 2:1–6. Jesus Christ is the foundation of our salvation. Each believer has the Spirit of God living within and like living stones, all believers together make up the church, the temple of the living God, in which God dwells by his Spirit. We have the responsibility to give attention to reading/hearing and obeying Scripture

with all our hearts. Obedience to God's Word is vital to spiritual transformation, because transformation takes place by means of the renewing of our minds through hearing and doing the Word of God.

The Scriptures reveal many ways of looking at and expressing the same truth, often through metaphor and story. Each Scripture passage listed above says similar things about what we are to do in order to achieve good outcomes in our lives.

To help you see the "To-Dos" in the above Scripture passages, on the lines below, write the Scripture reference for each one and then state in your own words what the verse says we "should" do. Then write the reason we should do them. (That's the "so that," or a similar phrase.)

As you break down the verses individually, you may find more than one "I Should" and "So That" within a given passage.

Here's an example:

Reference: Romans 12:1
I Should: offer myself as a living sacrifice to God
So That: I will be holy and pleasing to God and I will offer to God the worship that he deserves.

Here's another example:
Reference: Romans 12:2
I Should: not copy the ways and practices of this world, but instead be transformed by the renewing of my mind.
So That: I may test and discern what is the will of God.

Now you try it.
Reference: _____
I Should: _____
So That: _____

Reference: _____
I Should: _____
So That: _____

Reference: _____
I Should:_____
So That: _____

Reference: _____

I Should: _____

So That: _____

These are the practical out-workings of Jesus' teachings, the culmination of which is to love God supremely and love others as you want to be loved (read Matthew 7:7–12; Mark 12:28–31; Luke 6:31–36).

We learn about God and his ways by living in communion with other believers, reading/hearing/studying Scripture day after day, year after year, and relying on God's Spirit to teach us spiritual truths, as 1 Corinthians 2:10–13 states. When our reading of and obedience to Scripture is combined with teaching by God's Spirit, we are strengthened, and able to strengthen one another, to endure and to persevere through the difficulties of life, whether our difficulties be small or great.

Day 3
Walk This Way

1. Read Philippians 3:7–16.

   From the Word of God we learn how to live according to God's ways. We should strive to come to the point where we can personalize Paul's commitment to the Lord, making the goals he made for his life, our own.

   List below the commitments you make when you personalize Paul's words. The first one is given as an example.

Reference	I Will	For the Sake Of/So That
v. 7	count all as loss	Christ

Paul outlined in Philippians 3:7–14 the passion, focus, and direction of his entire life. This was the example he set for us to follow. Paul compared *knowing and obediently following Jesus* to *everything he owned and all he had achieved*, and he willingly gave up all those things for Jesus.

> Whatever things were gain to me, those things I have counted as loss for the sake of Christ. More than that, I count all things to be loss in view of the surpassing value of knowing Christ Jesus my Lord, for whom I have suffered the loss of all things, and count them but rubbish so that I may gain Christ. (Philippians 3:7–8)

2. Read Philippians 3:17; Colossians 3:1–4.

   Paul calls on us, his fellow believers, to follow his example of following Jesus Christ with full abandon. He also tells us to observe certain other believers' lives, to learn from and imitate them. What is it about their lives we are to observe? (v. 17)

   _____

Observers Observed

Observing is a two-way street. You are to observe and imitate those who live the way Paul did as he followed Christ. But keep in mind, others are observing, and possibly imitating, your life as well. Who are these people? They are the "generations" from Lesson 1 (Psalm 145)—everyone in your life. Let specific faces come before your mind's eye. Can those men and women, boys and girls safely imitate you in the way you follow Christ, patterning their lives after yours? On a scale from 1 to 10, write in a number to rate how strongly you would encourage others to imitate your life in the way you follow Christ, number 1 being the *least* encouraging (Don't Do as I Do) and 10 being *most* encouraging (Follow me …):

Don't Do As I Do   Follow Me the Way I Follow Christ

1_____5_____10

Day 4
Wrong Way! Do Not Enter

1. Read Philippians 3:18–19, quoted here:

   Many walk, of whom I often told you, and now tell you even weeping, that they are enemies of the cross of Christ, whose end is destruction, whose god is their appetite, and whose glory is in their shame, who set their minds on earthly things.

Following Paul's example of following Christ will give us the ability to discern between true followers/imitators of Christ and those who are false followers, who do not reflect Christ in their lifestyles—those who are, in fact, enemies of the cross of Christ.

Spend some time thinking about and praying through Philippians 3:7–14, 18–19. Humbly examine your own lifestyle, holding it up to Paul's pattern and example (vv. 7–14) and also to the examples of people who have their minds set on earthly things (vv. 18–19).

a. Closely study and contrast the *characteristics* and *consequences* of the way of life of those who live for earthly (temporal) things in vv. 18–19 with the *characteristics* and *consequences* of the life of Paul (Philippians 3:7–14), then list them below.

Minds Set On Earthly Things   Paul's Example

_____   _____
_____   _____
_____   _____
_____   _____
_____   _____
_____   _____
_____   _____
_____   _____

b. After a time of prayer before the Lord, mark where you believe your life/lifestyle falls on a scale between *those who have their minds set on earthly things* and *Paul's* life.

Mind On Earthly Things (vv. 18–19)   Life of Paul (vv. 7–14)

_____

c. Will you make the decision to move closer to following Paul's example of imitating Christ?

_____

To accomplish this goal, let's take a closer look at Paul's lifestyle and discover exactly what we are to do to follow his example.

2. Read Philippians 3:12–16, quoted here:

> ¹²Not that I have already obtained it or have already become perfect, but I press on so that I may lay hold of that for which also I was laid hold of by Christ Jesus. ¹³Brethren, I do not regard myself as having laid hold of it yet; but one thing I do: forgetting what lies behind and reaching forward to what lies ahead, ¹⁴I press on toward the goal for the prize of the upward call of God in Christ Jesus. ¹⁵Let us therefore, as many as are perfect, have this attitude; and if in anything you have a different attitude, God will reveal that also to you; ¹⁶however, let us keep living by that same standard to which we have attained.

Paul says two times that he is going to "press on" to do certain things. In verse 13 he says that pressing on is the "one thing" he does. This is Paul's single-minded focus.

a. There are two components to accomplishing that "one thing." What are they? (v. 13b)

_____

b. Revisit your resolution at the end of Lesson 1 to do the same things Paul says he did in Philippians 3:13–14. Are you forgetting the past and reaching forward to what lies ahead?

_____

If you keep practicing those things, as time passes they will become second nature. You cannot move forward while continuing to look back. Looking back is only productive for identifying God's gracious work in your life, praising him for it, and proclaiming the goodness of the Lord to others. Then you press on.

Jesus said ... "No one who puts his hand to the plow and looks back is fit for the kingdom of God" (Luke 9:62 HCSB).

Day 5
Hand on the Plow, Eyes Straight Ahead

1. What does it mean for us to "lay hold of that for which also I was laid hold of by Christ Jesus"? Look at the list you made of the characteristics of Paul's life (Day 4). Rewrite that list here:

_____

_____

_____

God isn't willy-nilly in the things he does and why he does them. He has a purpose in every action. God had specific things in view when he sent Jesus Christ into the world to redeem it. The death and resurrection of Jesus bought our redemption for a purpose. This purpose involves loving and obeying God with all we are and have, loving others, not living for the world and temporary things but being single-minded about our pursuit of God's ways and purposes, as Paul demonstrated so well.

2. We are to change our lifestyle to reflect this greater dimension of "pressing on" to be and do all that God redeemed us for. What are we supposed to be maintaining in our everyday lives as we do so (read Philippians 3:16 and 2 Peter 1:5–9)?

_____

_____

The past is gone. It must not define us today. Our identity is in Christ who redeemed us, whois making all things new, and who gave us his purposes for living.

What did you learn from the Scriptures in this lesson? Is there one Scripture that stands out? What is it?

_____

_____

What are you going to do about what you learned? Think about and write out your steps of obedience.

_____

_____

Resolve to:

1. Embrace what the Bible says about Jesus Christ (Matthew 16:15–17; Acts 4:10–12; 1 Peter 2:2).
2. Repent and receive God's forgiveness for past sins. Turn my back on my past and offer my life to God as a living sacrifice, living in his power (2Corinthians 5:17; Romans 12:1–2; Galatians 2:20; Philippians 3:7–14; 2 Peter 1:3–11).
3. Live up to what I have learned to this point about the truths of the Word of God (Psalm 19:7–14; 119:130; Matthew 5:17–19; 6:19–21; 22:36–39; and 28:18–20; John 15:8–10, 16–17; 1 Corinthians 2:10–13; 10:1–12; Philippians 3:16; 4:1).
4. Adopt the attitude of Paul, pressing on to be and do all that for which God redeemed me (Galatians 2:20; Philippians 3:12–14).

5. Set my mind on, and live for, what will last for eternity, not temporal, earthly things that will come to an end (Matthew 6:19–34; 16:21–25; Romans 8:29; 2 Corinthians 5:17; Ephesians 1:3–14; 2:1–10; 3:10–11; and 4:1, 17–24; Philippians 3:18–21; Colossians 3:1–3; Revelation 19:7–8; 21:2, 9–10).

6. Be an imitator of Jesus Christ, living my life before others as an example of a follower of Christ (Ephesians 5:1; Philippians 2:5–11, 3:17, 4:9; 1 Thessalonians 1:6, 7; 2:14; Hebrews 6:11–12; 11:8–10).

_____ (Initial here)

"The Rock! His work is perfect,
For all His ways are just;
A God of faithfulness and without injustice,
Righteous and upright is He." (Deuteronomy 32:4)

"All drank the same spiritual drink, for they were drinking from a spiritual rock which followed them; and the rock was Christ." (1 Corinthians 10:4)

"Therefore if anyone is in Christ, he is a new creature; the old things passed away; behold, new things have come." (2 Corinthians 5:17)

Lesson 3

Construction Zone

Day 1
Building on the Foundation

Read: *Brokenness to Beauty,* Part 2—The Bible

Chapter 8, "Building on the Foundation"
Read 1 Corinthians 3:10–15 every day this week. Choose at least one verse and memorize it.

> Foundations are of great importance, but they are not the whole building. It matters how I build my life and with what materials. (*Brokenness to Beauty*, 45)

Respond:

Once the foundation has been laid, the building can go up on it. How we build and the material we use are of utmost importance.

When we build a physical house on a foundation, or have others build on it for us, we expect a quality, finished product. And rightfully so. We don't want the walls falling on us in the slightest wind.

How much more important, therefore, should we build on the spiritual foundation of Jesus Christ using superior materials and methods. The quality of the foundation of our lives and that of the structure (our life) built on it aren't matters of temporal, physical well-being. They're matters of eternal, spiritual well-being.

1. Read 1 Corinthians 3:12–15. In these verses Paul writes about the one foundation of the church—Jesus Christ—and those who build on that foundation: ourselves and other teachers. These verses also speak of quality of materials, of workmanship, and of the end product in this building process.

   a. What material should we be using to build on the foundation of Jesus Christ? Jesus showed us the *material* to use and *how to use it* when he was confronted with the devil in the wilderness following his baptism:

      The tempter came and said to Him, "If You are the Son of God, command that these stones become bread." But He answered and said, *"It is written, 'Man shall not live on bread alone, but on every word that proceeds out of the mouth of God.'"* (Matthew 4:3–4, emphasis added)

      _____

   b. What did Jesus do when approached by the devil?

      _____

The Scripture that Jesus quoted from is what we call the Old Testament, and Jesus used a portion of Deuteronomy 8:3 to defeat his tempter. Jesus knew the Scripture, he loved and studied it, it was in his heart, and he built his life on it. As a result, he knew what was right. He was able to discern the lies of the tempter when he heard them, and he dealt appropriately with him, by quoting the Scripture that spoke directly to the lies of the enemy.

2. Read Matthew 4:5–7 and Psalm 91.

   a. The devil quoted Psalm 91:11–12. Write down the exact words he quoted to Jesus, recorded in Matthew 4:5–6.

      _____

   b. What phrase did the devil leave out of the verses he quoted?

      _____

Jesus correctly *interpreted* the Scriptures. He knew the Scriptures so he knew when the old deceiver misquoted Psalm 91:11–12. The devil deceptively left out "to guard you in all your ways" from verse 11, and he didn't go near verse 14, which reads, *"Because he has loved Me,* therefore I will deliver him... *because he has known My name"* (emphasis added). Jesus knew God would protect him "in all his ways" because he loved God, knew and honored his name, and walked in obedience to his Word.

Jesus knew the devil lifted verses out of the context in which they were written. The context of these verses is God's protection and deliverance of the man who "dwells in the shelter of the Most High," the man who says, "My God, in whom I trust!" (Psalm 91:1, 2).

God's promises are for those who love, trust, and fear him, whose ways are in obedience to God's Word. Those who insist on going their own way and doing their own thing, heedless of what God has said, cannot claim God's promises (read Isaiah 29:13–14; 58:1–2; 59:1–2; and James 4:1–4).

Additionally, Jesus correctly *applied* the Scriptures. He knew and quoted Deuteronomy 6:5 when he said, "On the other hand, you shall not put the LORD your God to the test." He knew we are not to play games with God or try to manipulate him to force his hand.

    c. With what material should we build on the foundation of our lives? (Matthew 4:4)

_____

    d. How did Jesus use that material? How should we use it?

_____

_____

From this passage we can see the value of regularly reading, meditating on, memorizing, and obeying the Bible, being "diligent to present yourself approved to God as a workman who does not need to be ashamed, accurately handling the word of truth" (1 Timothy 2:15). Not like the Pharisees did, as a matter of legalistic righteousness, but humbly, from the heart, with love for and reverence toward God. By these means, we will come to know God and his ways intimately, become familiar with what he has said, and allow his words to transform the way we think and act as we put them into practice.

God's words will also keep us from deadly error. Jesus demonstrated how to wield the powerful Sword of the Spirit, which is the Word of God. It enables us to discern between good and evil. We learn to know when we are being tempted with lies, regardless of how well they sound and how dressed-up they seem when they come to us; and we learn to understand how to refute the lies.

The Word of God is the material we use, and loving obedience to God's words is how we build on the foundation of Jesus Christ laid in our lives.

Day 2

Honorable Builders

1. Read Ephesians 4:11–13 and 14–16 and Hebrews 13:7, 17.

    What should we do when Bible teachers, authors, preachers, or pastors want to build on the foundation laid for our lives? They expect us to listen to and believe them, right? What is our responsibility?

    a. From the Ephesians verses above, what has God provided for us in the way of spiritually gifted people in the church? (Ephesians 4:11)

        _____

        _____

    b. What is the responsibility of these spiritual leaders, especially pastors and teachers? (Ephesians 4:12; Hebrews 13:17)

        _____

        _____

    c. What is our responsibility to godly spiritual leaders? (Hebrews 13:7; 1 Timothy 5:17–18; Galatians 6:6)

        _____

        _____

    d. Are you part of a Bible-teaching and -practicing local church? How are you carrying out your responsibility to your godly leaders?

        _____

        _____

Beware the Scammers

1. Read Matthew 7:15–23; 1 Timothy 4:1–2; 2 Peter 1:16–2:1; Hebrews 13:9; 1 John 4:1-3, and 3 John 9–10.

    Should we trust every teacher, preacher, author, or singer/songwriter who professes to speak God's truth, taking them at their word? Can we safely believe whatever is taught, or preached, or written by anyone who professes to speak in the name of God?

    _____

Just as we must beware of strangers who come to our door, or to our e-mail inbox, or call us on the phone to sell us good-sounding "deals," we should much more be wary of those who profess to speak for God and come to us with enticing words.

2. Read 1 Thessalonians 5:19–21.

What are two things Paul tells us to do when faced with teachings we are not certain about? (5:21)

_____

We are not to be hasty to reject teachings, for they may be from God. Nor are we to be hasty to accept what we hear, because it may not be from God, regardless of how appealing it may be. This is true whether the teaching comes from our own church pulpit or Bible study, or from those outside our local church. Test all things; hold tight to what is good and agrees with the teaching of Scripture.

How To "Examine Everything Carefully"

1. Read Acts 17:10–12.

What two things did the Berean Jews do after they first heard Paul preach in the synagogue, proclaiming that Jesus was the Christ? (17:11)

_____

_____

a. What do we learn from the Bereans about how we should examine teachings from preachers, speakers, authors, and songwriters who claim to speak the truth of God?

_____

The Bereans' examination of the Scriptures to determine whether this new teaching about Jesus being the Messiah was true resulted in their finding the truth about God's promised Messiah and receiving eternal life. A very positive outcome!

When the devil tempted him, Jesus' recall and correct understanding and use of Scripture were key to his continued obedience to the Father. He was thus able to fulfill the purpose for which he came into the world: to destroy the works of the devil and provide forgiveness of sins and salvation for all who will believe. He knew the truth, discerned lies, rejected the lies, and held tight to the truth.

In the same way, we are to examine every teaching we hear or read, using the Word of God to determine if those teachers and teachings are from God. We are to hold to the teachings that are true and reject those that are false.

Day 3
Holding Tight

1. Read 1 Timothy 1:4–6, 18–20; 4:12–16; and 6:20–21.

    a. What was Timothy to hold to, and what are we to hold to? (1:5, 19; 4:16)

    _____

    _____

    b. If we reject or neglect "a sincere faith" and "a good conscience," what might we suffer, as happened to Hymenaeus and Alexander when they did these things? (1:19)

    _____

    _____

    c. What was Paul's prescription for such behavior? (1:20)

    _____

    _____

    d. Does this sound like discipline we'd willingly choose for our lives?

    _____

    _____

    e. How do we avoid getting to the place these men were, whom Paul was compelled to discipline? (1:18, 19; 6:20)

    _____

    _____

    f. What was the clearly stated goal of the discipline Paul laid on these men? (1:20)

    _____

    _____

2. Read 1 Corinthians 3:10–15, quoted here from The Living Bible:

God, in his kindness, has taught me how to be an expert builder. I have laid the foundation and Apollos has built on it. But he who builds on the foundation must be very careful. And no one can ever lay any other real foundation than that one we already have—Jesus Christ. But there are various kinds of materials that can be used to build on that foundation. Some use gold and silver and jewels; and some build with sticks and hay or even straw! There is going to come a time of testing at Christ's Judgment Day to see what kind of material each builder has used. Everyone's work will be put through the fire so that all can see whether or not it keeps its value, and what was really accomplished. Then every workman who has built on the foundation with the right materials, and whose work still stands, will get his pay. But if the house he has built burns up, he will have a great loss. He himself will be saved, but like a man escaping through a wall of flames.

The above passage, as well as others, contains positive motivation to love and serve Christ wholeheartedly, and there is negative motivation as well!

Fire, when used properly, is of great benefit to humankind. But it can also cause great destruction, pain, and suffering. We frequently see fire used in Scripture as a metaphor for judgment. Here it symbolizes the testing of our life's end product, the structure we, and others have built on the foundation.

I don't want to be "like a man escaping through a wall of flames" when I stand before Christ. Do you?

We need to be on our guard against allowing false teachers to build on our life foundation. And we must be sure that as we construct (live out) our own life, we use the superior materials of the Bible and humble, loving obedience to the God of the Bible.

Putting a high priority on the Bible to transform us helps us guard against ending up where we never want to be: losing everything we lived for on earth and entering heaven scorched and shamed. Using the Scriptures rightly, putting them into practice as we live our lives day by day, will enable us to "receive a rich welcome into the eternal kingdom of our Lord and Savior Jesus Christ" (2 Peter 1:11 NIV).

What did you learn from this lesson? _____

What will you do about it?

_____

_____

Resolve to:

a. Build on the foundation of Jesus Christ laid in my life with the quality material of the Bible (Joshua 1:8; Psalm 119:11; Jeremiah 17:7–8; 1 Corinthians 3:10–15; Ephesians 6:17; 1 Thessalonians 2:13; Hebrews 5:11–14; James 1:21–27; 1 Peter 1:13–19).

b. Guard my heart from deceptive teachings, test all things by what the Bible states, hold tight to what it teaches (Proverbs 30:5–6; Isaiah 8:20; Acts 17:10–12; Acts 20:27–32; Romans 14:10–12; 16:17–19; 2 Corinthians 5:10, 14–15; 11:3–4, 13–15; Galatians 1:6–9; 1 Thessalonians 5:19–21; 2 Thessalonians 3:6–7, 14–15; 1 Timothy 1:3–5; 1 Timothy 4:1; 5:17–20; 6:12–21; 2 Timothy 3:10–17; Titus 1:15–2:1; Revelation 22:18–19).

_____ (Initial here)

"Look to God's instructions and teachings! People who
contradict his word are completely in the dark."
(Isaiah 8:20 NLT)

"Be diligent to present yourself approved to God as a workman who does
not need to be ashamed, accurately handling the word of truth."
(2Timothy 2:15)

Lesson 4

The Source of Hope

Day 1
Looking In All the Right Places

Read: *Brokenness to Beauty,* Part 2—The Bible

Chapter 2, "Finding Hope"
Chapter 5, "The Scriptures, Our Life"
Read Romans 15:4–5, 13 every day this week. Choose at least one verse and memorize it.

> Over the years I had learned to press on no matter how hard it became, even in the face of not knowing how things might turn out. But I leaned hard on God and his Word. The encouragement of the Scriptures is available to all, but it only comes from reading (or hearing) the Scriptures. (*Brokenness to Beauty,* 18)

Respond:

All of us need hope to move through life. We become especially aware of this when faced with circumstances beyond our control. When our lives are falling apart, where do we find hope to move ahead each day? What does the Bible have to do with producing hope in us? We will answer these questions in this study.

1. Early in Chapter 2 of *Brokenness to Beauty*, I recorded two responses I had when I learned I had breast cancer. When you have been faced with frightening situations, with circumstances beyond your control, and you were helpless to change anything yourself, what was your first response?

   _____

   Did you have a second response? What was it?

   _____

2. Read Joshua 1:1, 2, 5–9.

   What emotion did God speak directly to Joshua about when he tasked him with leading the Israelites into the land of Canaan? What words did God use? (v6, 7, 9)

   _____

   _____

3. Read Acts 17:33; 18:1, 4–10; and Acts 23:1, 6–11.

   a. When Paul was resisted and threatened for his witness about Jesus Christ what emotion did God speak directly to him about? What words did God use? Acts 18:9, 10; 23:11

      _____

      _____

   b. What common emotion did these men share, based on what the Lord told them? What methods did the Lord use to communicate with each man? (Joshua 1:6, 7, 9; Acts 18:9; 23:11)

      _____

      _____

   c. Joshua and Paul experienced extreme situations in their service of God, and God used special means to speak to them. How do you usually hear from God?

      _____

      _____

   d. Have you ever experienced a strong emotion such as fear?

      _____

      _____

e. Have you ever read a passage of Scripture and felt God spoke directly to you about that strong emotion or another issue?

_____

_____

f. How has that experience affected your view of the Bible?

_____

_____

God desires to speak to us, to calm our fears and lead us into the truth, so that we may better live for and serve him with joy and peace. We have to put ourselves in a position to hear him by regularly being in the Word, through which he speaks to us by his Spirit.

g. In Lesson 1 we learned an important truth from Scripture and resolved to make a lifestyle change: to read and think about God's Word regularly, reading daily, if possible. Are you doing that? If not, why not? What will you do to change that so you can better hear God?

_____

_____

Day 2
Learning From All the Right Places

1. Read Romans 15:4; 1 Corinthians 10:1–13.

a. What is one reason God had the Scriptures written down? (Romans 15:4a; 1 Corinthians 10:11)

_____

_____

b. 1 Corinthians 10:6–10 gives us a list of negative things to learn from what has been written in the Bible. List them here.

_____

_____

c. What two positive things should we learn from what is written in the Bible? (Rom. 15:4b)

_____

_____

d. What is the outcome of learning to persevere and gaining encouragement from the Scriptures? (Rom. 15:4b)

_____

_____

Romans 15:4 states we should learn two crucial things from reading the Scriptures: endurance and encouragement. The ultimate result, the fruit of learning to endure and being encouraged by the Scriptures is hope, even in our scary and out-of-our-control circumstances.

2. Read Romans 15:5 and 15:13, both quoted here:

Now may the God who gives perseverance and encouragement … (v.5)
Now may the God of hope fill you with all joy and peace in believing, so that you will abound in hope by the power of the Holy Spirit. (v.13)

a. Who is the source and supplier of endurance/perseverance and encouragement? (v. 5)

_____

_____

_____

b. Who is the source of hope? By whose power are we able to abound in hope? (v. 13)

_____

_____

_____

Reading the Bible, being instructed by God, and putting his word into practice, is pivotal in our decision to praise God in unwanted circumstances.

c. Hope in the midst of our circumstances should cause us to praise God together with our fellow believers (Romans 15:4–6). Are you doing that regularly?

_____

_____

_____

d. Look back at the time-line of your life in Lesson 1. Identify a time when you know you learned something about persevering, and a time when you were encouraged to press on by what you read in the Bible. Make a special mark at that place on the time-line. Take a moment to thank God for his love and care of you by speaking to you through his Word, teaching and encouraging you. Write your prayer of thanks here.

_____

_____

_____

Share your praise with another believer, perhaps someone in this study with you.

3. Read Psalm 50:14–15, 23 and Romans 15:5–6.

a. When you praise God, giving him thanks, especially when done together with other believers, what are you ultimately doing?

_____

_____

_____

Our God is the God of endurance and encouragement and hope, and he is worthy of our praise and thanks. *We* may not be in control, but *he* is. In the above verses, we discover three key factors for finding hope:

*   Learning from and obeying the Scriptures, which were written to instruct us.
*   Learning endurance and gaining encouragement from God through his Word.
*   Receiving joy, peace, and hope from the God of hope.

When these three converge, they produce a "perfect storm" of hope making in us! We overflow with hope by his power through his Spirit. Hope grounded in the God of Hope.

Day 3
Lifelong Learners

As we read the Bible day after day we learn from the true life stories of others, from their errors as well as their right choices (1 Corinthians 10:6–11). We learn who God is, what he is like, what is important to him, how he has dealt with those who fear, honor, and obey him, as well as how he has dealt with those who refuse to fear, honor, and obey him.

1. Again referring to your time-line in Lesson 1, pick one incident you identified as a time when you recognized God was working in your circumstances, turning a negative situation into a positive one. Briefly write that story here.

_____
_____
_____
_____
_____
_____

2. Think of a biblical story that closely compares to your story, has similar elements or an outcome like the one you experienced. If you cannot think of one, discuss with others in the group or another Christian friend what Bible story might compare to yours. Write the Bible reference (where in the Bible you find the story) and briefly show the comparison to your story here.

_____
_____
_____
_____
_____
_____

Learning is a process, a lifelong journey. It has its starting point at our choice to make time for listening to and communing with God (primarily through his Word and prayer). We maintain it by the choice we make every day to humbly learn from God's Word, putting it into practice in our lives.

Day 4
Learning to Live

We are encouraged to read the Bible and do what it says not because it is a nice idea, a good way among many ways. No, the Scriptures are unique. They are God's words to us. They are alive, powerful, and eternal. What God says he will do, he does. We can stake our lives on it. In fact, taking heed to the words of God is the only way to live—literally.

1. Read Deuteronomy 30:15–20. Listen in on Moses' final warning to the Israelites. Now read Deuteronomy 32:46–47, quoted here (emphasis added):

He said to them, "Take to your heart all the words with which I am warning you today, which you shall command your sons to observe carefully, even all the words of this law. *For it is not an idle word for you; indeed it is your life.* And by this word you will prolong your days in the land, which you are about to cross the Jordan to possess."

a. Moses' words in Deuteronomy 30:15–20 offer two choices. What are these choices?

    _____

b. To choose life, what did the Israelites have to do?

    _____

c. To choose death, what did the Israelites have to do?

    _____

d. Do you think God's Word has become less important over time? Is it less weighty for us today than for the Israelites in Moses' day?

    _____

e. What did Jesus say about the importance of God's words? (Matthew 4:3–4)

    _____

f. What were the apostles' and early church leaders' belief about God's Word? (James 1:22)

    _____

g. For us to choose life, what must we do? (Matthew 7:24–25)

    _____

h. For us to choose death, what must we do, or not do? (Matthew 7:26–27)

    _____

The words of God are our life, as surely as they were the life of Israel. Jesus said, "Man shall not live on bread alone, but on every word that proceeds out of the mouth of God" (Matthew 4:4). Those words are not figurative but literal. To disregard and disobey God's Word is to choose the way of death, but obedience to the Word of God is the way of life.

i. The Word of God is the source of life, strength, and encouragement that we can hold on to, especially in our times of desperate struggle. God's Word will never fail us. Do you believe we need this source of life, strength, and encouragement all of our days, not just when we are in desperation and are aware that we need it?

_____

2. Do you have a favorite Scripture verse or passage that you keep going to when times get rough? What is it? (If you don't have one, go to Psalm 25 at the back of this lesson and read it for this exercise.)

_____

   a. What is it that speaks to you in those verses?

   _____

   _____

   b. What have these verses taught you about God? About yourself?

   _____

   _____

   c. Did you change your thinking and behavior based on those truths? If so, what changed?

   _____

   _____

   Have you carried over into your "good" days the truths you learned from the Word of God during the "bad" days, the hard times in your life? If not, take time now to look up those favorite verses, meditate on them before the Lord, repent, and make up your mind to obey them every day, not just when you are in desperate need. God's words are your life.

   Psalm 25

   To You, O Lord, I lift up my soul.
   O my God, in You I trust, do not let me be ashamed; do not let my enemies exult over me.
   Indeed, none of those who wait for You will be ashamed; those who deal treacherously without cause will be ashamed.
   Make me know Your ways, O Lord; teach me Your paths.
   Lead me in Your truth and teach me, for You are the God of my salvation; for You I wait all the day.
   Remember, O Lord, Your compassion and Your lovingkindnesses, for they have been from of old.

Do not remember the sins of my youth or my transgressions; according to Your lovingkindness remember me, for Your goodness' sake, O Lord.
Good and upright is the Lord; therefore He instructs sinners in the way.
He leads the humble in justice, and He teaches the humble His way.
All the paths of the Lord are lovingkindness and truth to those who keep His covenant and His testimonies.
For Your name's sake, O Lord, pardon my iniquity, for it is great.
Who is the man who fears the Lord? He will instruct him in the way he should choose.
His soul will abide in prosperity, and his descendants will inherit the land.
The secret of the Lord is for those who fear Him, and He will make them know His covenant.

What did you learn from this lesson?

_____

What will you do about it?

_____

Resolve to:

a. Allow the Word of God to instruct and encourage me as I read it (Psalm 119:105; Romans 15:4–5; 1 Corinthians 10:1–12).
b. Adopt the biblical perspective that suffering is a means to endurance, character, and hope (Psalm 119:67; Romans 5:1–5; Hebrews 12:4–11).
c. Treat the Word of God as it truly is, "my life," in the bad days and the good days, living it out all the days of my life (Deuteronomy 27 and 28; Deuteronomy 32:46, 47; Proverbs 4:20–23; Matthew 7:24–27; 4:7; Philippians 2:12–13).

_____ (Initial here)

"Many of His disciples withdrew and were not walking with Him anymore. So Jesus said to the twelve, 'You do not want to go away also, do you?' Simon Peter answered Him, 'Lord, to whom shall we go? You have words of eternal life.'"
(John 6:66–68)

"Open my eyes, that I may behold
Wonderful things from Your law."
(Psalm 119:18)

Lesson 5

Listening, Trusting, Seeing

Day 1
Listening to God

Read: *Brokenness to Beauty*, Part 2—The Bible

Chapter 4, "God Calls Us"
Chapter 6, "Trusting God"
Chapter 7, "Perspective Is Everything"
Read Hebrews 12:1–13 every day this week. Choose at least one verse and memorize it.

> Times of trial can be opportunities to turn to God and reach out to him as never before. Those who do ... find grace for the difficulties. In God there is strength, comfort, and his presence with us through the dark valleys. (*Brokenness to Beauty*, 29)

Respond:
Hearing God's Call

1. Read Isaiah 65:2.

    God is always calling to us, as he called to Israel. They were not listening. Are we?

   a. In our culture we tend to race through our days in a blur of activity. Have you ever said or thought these things below?

      *   I don't have time for reading the Bible. _____
      *   I don't have time for prayer. _____
      *   I don't have time for (fill in the blank) _____

   Even if we haven't said or consciously thought these things, our lifestyles demonstrate whether we live our lives listening to God or "walk in the way that is not good," ignoring him and going our own way, just as Israel did. What could make us slow down and listen?

   C. S. Lewis, in his book, *The Problem of Pain*, indicated that when life is going well we tend not to depend on God but steam along on our own power, ignoring him. In light of that tendency, God will often interrupt our lives with unpleasantness to get our attention so we will look to him and learn what is truly important in life.[1]

   b. Has anything unexpected or unwanted entered your life and slowed you down?

   _____

   There is nothing like abject fear, pain, or a sense of powerlessness to drive us to our knees, crying out for help from someone who is not overwhelmed by any of the things that overwhelm us.

   c. If you are in that place, are you ready to cry out to God, who is able to help you through your time of darkness and need? He's been calling to you.

   _____

   Many women and men, stopped cold, lying flat on their faces cried out to God. They were in the right place to hear God calling. And when they turned and called out to him, they realized he was already there.

2. Read Psalm 28:1–2, 6–7, quoted below:

   To You, O Lord, I call; my rock, do not be deaf to me, for if You are silent to me, I will become like those who go down to the pit. Hear the voice of my supplications when I cry to You for help. … Blessed be the Lord, because He has heard the voice of my supplication. The Lord is my strength and my shield; my heart trusts in Him, and I am helped; therefore my heart exults, and with my song I shall thank Him.

a. Note the progression of action in those verses. Circle the phrases in the text that coincide with the steps listed below:

- He cried out to God for help.
- God heard his prayer.
- He trusted in God.
- God helped him.
- He rejoiced and thanked God.

b. What can you learn from the psalmist's journey that you can apply to your own journey through trials?

_____

_____

_____

Use this kind of exercise with other Psalms to see what you can learn from them as you travel through trials. They were written for that purpose, to instruct us, so that we might gain encouragement and learn to persevere.

3. Read Psalm 119:67 and 71, quoted here:

Before I was afflicted I went astray, but now I keep your word.
It is good for me that I was afflicted, that I might learn your statutes.

a. Based on your reading of Psalm 28 (above in #2) and these verses from Psalm 119 (above in #3), what good would you say could come from suffering?

_____

_____

_____

God can redeem any frightening or overwhelming situation, turning it into the means of getting our attention so that he can teach us his ways. As just one example of good coming out of suffering—it can stop us in our busyness and remind us to listen to the voice of God as he calls to us. If we turn to God and cry out to him, we will find him already there, "a very present help in trouble" (Psalm 46:1).

Drawing close to God in times of need begins a process of learning more about him … and about our own selves. Confession follows naturally, as we learn the ways of God revealed in his Word. We begin to understand the value of the Word of God and walking in loving obedience to him. Then we can truthfully say to him, "Your statutes are my songs in the house of my pilgrimage" (Psalm 119:54).

Read: Deuteronomy 8:2–3; Hebrews 12:1–13.

Day 2
Trusting God

1. Read Psalm 37:3–6.

    a. What are you trusting God for these days?

    _____
    _____
    _____

    b. What are you *not* trusting God for these days? In other words, what are you worrying about? Or are you trusting in something, someone, or even yourself, *rather than* trusting in God? Take time to analyze in what area of your life you are not trusting God. Write it here:

    _____
    _____
    _____

2. Read Philippians 4:6–9.

    a. What are we told *not* to do?

    _____
    _____
    _____

    b. Why do you suppose we are commanded not to be anxious?

    _____
    _____
    _____

    c. What does our worry reveal about our understanding of and relationship with God?

    _____
    _____
    _____

d. What are we told *to do*? (Rephrase in your own words.)

_____

_____

_____

e. What is the promised result?

_____

_____

_____

Worry, anxiety, and fear are the antitheses, the absolute opposites, of trusting in God. These emotions give the lie to our statement that we are acting in faith, making it obvious we are not.

We all struggle with worry, anxiety, and fear. That's why Paul wrote Philippians 4:6–9! When we find ourselves battling those emotions, we can go to God and

- stop our anxious thoughts,
- start thinking the right things, and
- receive God's peace.

f. If you need to give up some worries, fears, or even give up trusting in something other than God, write it here:

_____

_____

_____

g. Now give the anxious thoughts, fears, and control of your life to God. Then follow through and thank him, intentionally thinking on the things Paul lists in verses 8 and 9. Write your prayer here:

_____

_____

_____

Read: Psalm 55:22; 1 Peter 5:6–7; Matthew 6:11, 19–34.

Day 3
Perspective Is Everything—Seeing Correctly

Perspective: "a particular way of regarding something."[2]
Our way of seeing something is of vital importance in the midst of difficulties. Though our perspective may not determine the outcome of our situation, it will

determine the quality of our journey through the difficulties, whatever form they may take.

1. Read Psalm 121:1–2 and Psalm 95:3–5.

   a. How might the act of lifting up our physical eyes to the mountains or something else in God's creation help us lift up our spiritual eyes, giving us a different perspective on the looming circumstances we face?

   _____

   _____

   b. What has helped you shift your eyesight from your problems to God, the one who is your source of help?

   _____

   _____

   c. Perspective shift: Since the Lord made the mountains, indeed the whole world, do you believe he can help you face the mountain of your troubles?

   _____

   _____

   When the psalmist looked up and saw the mighty, majestic mountains, his spiritual eyes recognized the source of his help: the Lord, who made those mountains.

   d. How do you think we can get to the place of "seeing the Lord" when we "look up," as the psalmist did?

   _____

   _____

2. Read Deuteronomy 29:29, Luke 24:13–27, John 5:39, and Hebrews 1:1–3.

   a. What does Deuteronomy 29:29 tell us about Scripture?

   _____

   _____

   b. What does Luke 24:13–2 tell us about Scripture? About Jesus?

   _____

   _____

c. What does John 5:39 tell us about Scripture? About Jesus?

_____

_____

d. What does Hebrews 1:1–3 tell us about Scripture? About Jesus?

_____

_____

Learning *who God is* and *what he does* is crucial to "seeing" the Lord. When we see the God of the Bible, and recognize that he is the one who helps us, we see our problems differently. They may loom like a mountain in front of us, but we know God is bigger than our greatest problem; in fact, he is sovereign over that mountain of trouble. Now, that's perspective.

e. Take a moment to turn your spiritual eyes to the God who is greater than the mountains he created, to the God who is sovereign over your life and your problems. Focus on him rather than on your difficulties. Worship the God Who Is. Write down your prayer of adoration here:

_____

_____

Day 4
Dying to Live

The Scriptures give us a right perspective on life and our struggles by revealing who God is and what he does. The Scriptures also teach us to center our lives in God and his purposes, not in ourselves and our desires apart from him. When we center our lives in ourselves, we run into trouble with self-pity. And make no mistake, self-pity is sin. Self-pity is filled with deadly poison. And like a viper, it must be dealt the death blow swiftly.

1. Read Numbers 14:1–23 and Philippians 2:14–15.

a. What can we learn about how God views grumbling and complaining against his care and provision for us? (Numbers 14)

_____

_____

We would do well to learn a lesson from the Israelites, complainers and self-pitiers who were not satisfied with God's gracious provision and mighty works done on their behalf. God called their complaining and rejection rebellion against him.

Self-pity is a perverse focus on oneself. It demands fulfillment of our desires irrespective of the gracious working of God on our behalf. It produces complaining, poisons others to join us, stirs up the anger of God against us, and brings down his judgment upon us! Self-pity is not the way of God. It is the way of the flesh and must be put to death with the rest of our old nature.

b. Whose people and what sort of people will we prove ourselves to be if we are not complainers and disputers? (Philippians 2:14–15)

_____

_____

2. Read Ephesians 4:22–24, quoted here:

In reference to your former manner of life, you lay aside the old self, which is being corrupted in accordance with the lusts of deceit, and that you be renewed in the spirit of your mind, and put on the new self, which in the likeness of God has been created in righteousness and holiness of the truth.

a. Take a moment to search your heart for any shred of self-pity and self-centeredness. Confess these as sin and repent, turning your back on them and turning toward God to live in his likeness of righteousness and holiness of the truth. Write your prayer of repentance and thanksgiving to God.

_____

_____

_____

_____

_____

3. Read 1 Corinthians 10:1–6, 7–11; Colossians 3:1–11, 12–17; Ephesians 1:18–20; 3:16.

a. When we read Scripture, what are things we should be looking for (1 Cor. 10: 6, 11)?

_____

_____

_____

_____

_____

b. List the things Paul says we should learn NOT to do. (1 Cor. 10:6–10 and Colossians 3:5, 8, 9).

_____

_____

_____

_____

_____

c. *What* are the things we are *to do* instead? (Colossians 3:1–2, 10, 12–17)

_____

_____

_____

_____

_____

d. *Why* are we to do these things? (Col. 3:1, 3, 4, 10–12a, 15b)

_____

_____

_____

_____

e. *How* are we are able to do them? (Col. 3:1–4, 10–12a, 15–17; Ephesians 1:19–20; 3:16)

_____

_____

_____

_____

I have been crucified with Christ; and it is no longer I who live, but Christ lives in me; and the life which I now live in the flesh I live by faith in the Son of God, who loved me and gave Himself up for me. (Galatians 2:20)

Read: Romans 6:6–13; 1 Corinthians 10:10; Ephesians 4:20–5:21; Philippians 2:14–15; 4:6–9; 2 Timothy 3:16, 17; Jude 16.

Day 5
Nothing Wasted

Work through the "Growth through Crisis Worksheet" located after Lesson 10.

What did you learn from this lesson?

_____

What will you do about it?

_____

Resolve to:

    a. Slow down to take time to listen for God's voice in his Word and humbly obey him (Psalm 57; 92:1–2; Isaiah 65:2; Hebrews 4:1, 2, 6, 7, 10–16).

    b. Trust God rather than worry or depend on myself (or anyone or anything else), bringing all my fears and anxieties to him, change my thinking patterns and receive his peace (Psalm 37:3–7; 55:22; Philippians 4:6–9; 1 Peter 5:5–7).

    c. Learn who God is through his Word so as to gain the proper perspective as I go through life, in trials and good days alike (Romans 12:1–2).

    d. Put to death all self-pity, treating it for what it is, rebellion against God, and walk in newness of life in Christ Jesus (Romans 6:11; Ephesians 4:22–24; 5:1, 8–10).

_____ (Initial here)

"When I am afraid, I will put my trust in You.
In God, whose word I praise, in God I have put my trust;
I shall not be afraid. What can mere man do to me?"
(Psalm 56:3–4)

Lesson 6

Words and Hearts

Day 1
It's What's Inside That Counts

Read: *Brokenness to Beauty,* Part 3—Prayer

Chapter 9, "Like a Child"
Chapter 10, "Types of Prayer"
Chapter 11, "Prayer—Just Do It"
Read Matthew 5:1–20 and Isaiah 57:15 every day this week and choose at least one verse to memorize.

> Approaching God by focusing my attention on him, worshiping and adoring him, gave me a whole new perspective on prayer, and on my whole Christian life. (*Brokenness to Beauty*, 75)

Respond:

Prayer is something every Christian is supposed to know about and practice. And yet, many Christians feel inadequate when it comes to praying.

1. Describe your feelings about prayer.

   _____

   _____

The reality is, we aren't born (or born again) with a complete understanding of prayer. We grow in our understanding of prayer by praying with other believers and learning about prayer in the Bible.

2. How did you learn to pray?

_____

_____

For the most part, we learn how to pray by
a. observing other Christians pray and hearing them talk about prayer,
b. reading the prayers in the Bible, and
c. finally, we learn to pray by praying.

3. How would you define prayer; what is it?

_____

_____

In prayer, we communicate with God. He speaks to us in his Word and by his Spirit; we speak to him in prayer. Prayer is our side of conversing with God. Let's look at these aspects of prayer:
a. how to relate to God,
b. our spirits, and
c. our words.

4. Read John 4:23–24, quoted here (emphasis added):

But an hour is coming, and now is, when the true worshipers will worship the Father in spirit and truth; for such people the Father seeks to be His worshipers. *God is spirit, and those who worship Him must worship in spirit and truth.* Words are important in the communication process, but prayer is more than words. Since prayer is closely linked with worship, let's see what can we learn about prayer from this passage of Scripture about worshiping God.

a. What does Jesus teach us about God (v. 24)?

_____

b. What does Jesus say about how we are to worship God (v. 24)?

_____

c. What kind of worshipers does our heavenly Father seek (v. 23)?

_____

d. How would worshiping God in spirit and truth affect how we pray?

_____

Jesus quoted the prophet Isaiah (Isaiah 29:13) to the Pharisees: "This people honors Me with their lips, *but their heart is far away from Me*" (Mark 7:6, emphasis added).

5. Based on what you just learned about what God desires in those who worship him, how do you think God felt about those who worshiped him with their words but not their hearts? (Mark 7:6, 7)

_____

6. Do you think God views our words and hearts any differently when we pray from when we worship?

_____

7. Based on the previous Scriptures, what does the omniscient (all-knowing) God listen and respond to when we pray, our words or our hearts?

_____

We cannot pretend with God. We do not need to impress him and, in fact, *cannot* impress him with eloquent words. Nor do we disappoint him with halting, stumbling words. It is through our spirits, our hearts that we communicate with God's Spirit, in prayer as in worship. He listens and responds to our hearts and knows what we really mean.

Day 2
The Way Up Is Down

1. Read Micah 6:8, Matthew 18:4, and Luke 18:9–17.

    a. What one word from these verses clarifies how we are to relate to God, not just in prayer and worship, but also in all of life?

    _____

2. Read Matthew 6:9–15.

    a. In what way does the opening of the Lord's prayer, "Our Father, who is in heaven, hallowed be Your name," reflect humility on the part of the one praying?[3]

    _____

b. Who is the focus of attention in this opening?

_____

c. List the things we can learn about God from each of these phrases in this opening to prayer.
Our Father Who is in heaven: _____
Hallowed be Your name: _____

3. Work through the rest of the Lord's prayer this way, phrase by phrase. You will learn more *about God* and about *yourself* and *how you should relate to God and to others*. Record these findings for each phrase. Write down any other verses that come to mind that shed light on these phrases.

Your kingdom come:

_____

_____

Your will be done:

_____

_____

On earth as it is in heaven:

_____

_____

Give us this day our daily bread:

_____

_____

And forgive us our debts, as we also have forgiven our debtors:

_____

_____

And do not lead us into temptation, but deliver us from evil:

_____

_____

For Yours is the kingdom and the power and the glory forever. Amen.

_____

_____

4. Read 1 Chronicles 29:9–20 and Isaiah 6:1–9.

    a. In the left column, list the words applied to God; for example, "Blessed are
        you (1 Chronicles 29:10)." In the right column, list what we can *learn about
        ourselves* and/or *what we should do*; for example, "Who am I? (29:14)."
        1 Chronicles 29:9–20

Words About God	Words About Us/What We Should Do
_____	_____
_____	_____
_____	_____
_____	_____
_____	_____

    Isaiah 6:1–9

Words About God	Words About Us/What We Should Do
_____	_____
_____	_____
_____	_____
_____	_____
_____	_____

5. Read these passages: 1 Chronicles 29:10–15 and Isaiah 6:5–9.

    a. List the reasons King David and Isaiah responded as they did. What did they
        believe about God and about themselves that made them say what they said?
        (See your lists above.)

        _____

        _____

    b. Would you say their attitudes toward God were humble? What other words
        come to mind to describe David and Isaiah's attitude toward God? (Example:
        respectful.)

        _____

        _____

    It is clear from these Scriptures that in prayer, the attitude of our hearts is
    important to God.

Day 3
Words—A Window On the Heart

Prayer involves our words to God, but prayer is more than words, as we are discovering. Prayer involves our heart attitude toward God, which should be one of humility and truthfulness. Though we cannot impress God with our words, our words are still important—not just when we direct them to God in prayer, but at all times.

1. Re-read 1 Chronicles 29:10–13. Keeping in mind the words David spoke to God, consider your own words *to* God and your words *about* God. Are they humble and heartfelt, as David's were?

   _____

What's In A Name?

2. Re-read Matthew 6:9.

   a. Fill in the missing words: Hallowed be _____

   b. What are we to hallow, to consider holy and blessed?

   _____

   Using a Bible concordance, look up the word "name." Go to the lists of Psalms and the prophetic books. Choose five verses that refer to the name of God and write, below, what each verse reveals about his name. If you do not have a concordance, choose five verses from different Psalms that speak about the name of God.

   We are not dealing here with the *names of God*, such as Jehovah-Jireh, which describe attributes or actions of God. We are looking for the Scriptures that simply describe *the name of God*, such as we see in Psalm 103:1 below.

Book of the Bible and Verse	What Is Revealed About the Name of God
Example: Psalm 103:1	His name is holy
1. _____	_____
2. _____	_____
3. _____	_____
4. _____	_____
5. _____	_____

1. Summarize what these five verses teach us about the name of God.

   _____

   _____

   a. Did any of these verses shed new light for you on God and his name?

      _____

      _____

   b. What did you learn?

      _____

      _____

Discernment Comes from Knowing Truth

1. In light of what we've read in the Bible (these five verses about the name of God and David and Isaiah's prayers), what do you suppose God thinks about such expressions as "Oh my God," or using Lord, God, or Jesus Christ's name in our exclamations in everyday speech?

   _____

   _____

2. What do these expressions reveal about our hearts and about what we believe about God's name?

   _____

   _____

3. Read Exodus 20:7, quoted here:

   > You shall not take the name of the Lord your God in vain, for the
   > Lord will not leave him unpunished who takes His name in vain.

Jesus said, "A good man out of the good treasure of his heart brings forth good things, and an evil man out of the evil treasure brings forth evil things. But I say to you that *for every idle word men may speak, they will give account of it in the day of judgment*" (Matthew 12:35–36 NKJV, emphasis added).

James wrote "No one can tame the tongue; it is a restless evil and full of deadly poison. With it we bless our Lord and Father, and with it we curse men, who have been made in the likeness of God; from the same mouth come both blessing and cursing. My brethren, these things ought not to be this way" (James 3:8–10).

a. What do these verses clearly teach about the way we use our words, and the consequences, both in speaking about God and about others?

_____

_____

_____

_____

Our heart attitude toward God is extremely important. What is in our hearts will come out of our mouths. How we use God's name reveals what is in our hearts.

b. Will God simply look the other way when we use his name lightly and inappropriately? (Exodus 20:7)

_____

c. Will God hold us accountable for how we use his name? (Exodus 20:7)

_____

d. Should we say out of the same mouth good things about God and bad things about another person? (Ephesians 4:29; James 3:8–10)

_____

There is a day coming when all people will stand before God and be judged for what they've said and done in the body. This applies to those who do not know or love God and his Son Jesus Christ (Revelation 20:11–15), and those who do know, love, and serve God through faith in his Son Jesus Christ (2 Corinthians 5:10; 1 Corinthians 3:10–17).

God is compassionate, gracious, and forgiving. He says, "Today" is the day of salvation, the day to enter into my salvation rest (Hebrews 4). For followers of Jesus Christ, Today is the day to repent of and forsake sin in our lives, moving forward to live whole-heartedly for Christ.

If God's Spirit has convicted you of anything that you need to eliminate from your life in order to make your heart right with God, take time right now to repent and seek his forgiveness. If there are things you need to change and start doing, make that commitment to God now (Hebrews 4:1–11; 12:1–2; 1 John 1:8–9; Proverbs 28:13). Write your prayer.

_____

_____

_____

_____
_____
_____

For the high and exalted One
He who inhabits eternity,
Whose name is Holy says this,
"I dwell on the high and holy place,
But also with the contrite and humble in spirit
In order to revive the spirit of the humble
And to revive the heart of the contrite [overcome with sorrow for sin]."
(Isaiah 57:15 AMP)

Day 4
Hold the Line

The question before us now is, how do I keep going in the right direction, doing what is right, not what is wrong, in what I say and in every part of my life?

1. Read each passage of Scripture listed below. Look for these three items and record your findings if they are within the given passage:

    a. what has taken place to change our lives,
    b. the things we are *to do* or *not to do*, and
    c. by what power we are able to do them.

Romans 6:1–13

_____
_____
_____
_____
_____

Galatians 5:22–26

_____
_____
_____
_____
_____

Ephesians 4:20–25, 29, 32

_____

_____

_____

_____

_____

Ephesians 5:1–2; 6:10–18

_____

_____

_____

_____

_____

Philippians 1:27; 2:2–13

_____

_____

_____

_____

_____

Colossians 3:15–17

_____

_____

_____

_____

_____

2. Summarize in a few lines what you discovered from the above verses that answer these three questions:

   a. What has taken place to change our lives?
   b. What are the things we are *to do* or *not to do*?
   c. By what power we are able to do them?

   _____

   _____

   _____

   _____

d. The key, Jesus said, is to remain (abide) in him. What does that mean? How do we do it?
   John 15:4, 7, 10.

   _____

   _____

   _____

   _____

   _____

Move forward in hot pursuit of Jesus Christ, learning from those who have gone before you—like David, Isaiah, and Paul—to walk in humility before God and with men, reverencing God and his name. Pray with:

- humility toward God,
- confidence in God, and
- the power of God.

   Turn to Me and be saved, all the ends of the earth; for I am God, and there is no other. I have sworn by Myself, the word has gone forth from My mouth in righteousness and will not turn back, that to Me every knee will bow, every tongue will swear allegiance.
   (Isaiah 45:22–23)

   God highly exalted Him, and bestowed on Him the name which is above every name, so that at the name of Jesus every knee will bow, of those who are in heaven and on earth and under the earth, and that every tongue will confess that Jesus Christ is Lord, to the glory of God the Father. (Philippians 2:9–11)

What one or two things did you learn from this lesson?

_____

What steps of obedience will you take based on what you learned?

_____

Resolve to:

a. Come to God humbly, in sincerity of heart, honoring and worshiping him as sovereign God and Lord of my life (1 Chronicles 29:10–20; 2 Chronicles

6:1–7:3; Psalm 119:9–11; Micah 6:8; Hebrews 11 and 12; 1 Peter 5:5–6; 2 Peter 1:3–11; 3:18).

b. Reverence (fear) God and his name as holy, obeying him and blessing him with my words, guarding my heart and my tongue, choosing to bless other people rather than curse them by bad talk about them (Deuteronomy 10:12–13; Psalm 15; 48:10; 99:3; 135:13; Proverbs 4:23; Jeremiah 17:9–10; Malachi 3:16–18; Galatians 6:7–8; Ephesians 4:29).

c. Quickly repent of all that God's Spirit convicts me of, choosing God's compassion rather than his judgment (Proverbs 4:4, 11–13, 23; and 28:13; Ecclesiastes 12:13–14; 2 Corinthians 5:20–21; 6:1–4).

d. Learn to walk in the Spirit, abiding in Christ, not doing what my flesh/old nature/old self wants to do, but doing what God desires me to do (John 15:4; Galatians 5:22–25; 6:7–8; Ephesians 4:20–24).

e. Learn more about prayer by studying the prayers in Scripture, praying the prayers of Scripture, and praying with men and women of prayer (Proverbs 28:9; Matthew 6:5–15; John 14:12–20, 26; 16:5–13, 23–27; 1 Timothy 2:1–4, 5–6, 8; James 5:13–20; 1 John 5:14–15).

_____ (Initial)

"May the words of my mouth
and the meditation of my heart
be acceptable to You, Lord,
my rock and my Redeemer."
(Psalm 19:14 HCSB)

Lesson 7

Faith Is A Verb

Day 1
Faith Acts

Read: *Brokenness to Beauty,* Part 3—Prayer

    Chapter 12, Prayer as Relationship
    Chapter 13, Prayer as Our Lifeline
    Chapter 14, Orientation for Prayer
Read Hebrews 11:1–6 every day this week. Choose at least one verse and memorize it.

> Our faith in God is not just in what he can do, but in himself, who he is. What God does comes out of who he is. This is where our faith must take root—believing that God is who he says he is. ... Trust in God must be cultivated. It must become the bedrock from which we pray. (*Brokenness to Beauty,* 80–81)

Respond:

Though there are many facets of prayer, its foundation is faith in God and in what he says.

> Now faith is *the assurance* of things hoped for, *the conviction* of things not seen. For by it the men of old *gained approval.* ... By faith

> Enoch was taken up so that he would not see death; and he was not found because God took him up; for he obtained the witness that before his being taken up *he was pleasing to God. And without faith it is impossible to please Him, for he who comes to God must believe that He is and that He is a rewarder of those who seek Him.* (Hebrews 11:1–2, 5–6, emphasis added)

Faith sees and acts on what can only be seen with the spiritual eye, not the physical eye. Our relationship with God is all about faith. We cannot see him with our physical eyes but we *believe* he exists, we *believe* what he has said, and we *act* on that belief (Hebrews 11:6). That is living by faith. The entire eleventh chapter of Hebrews shows us what faith lived out looks like.

1. Read Hebrews 11:1–6, Romans 1:4–5, Romans 16:25–27, and James 2:14–23.

    a. The Bible uses the phrase "the obedience of faith" or "the obedience that comes from faith" (NIV). What do you think that means, based on the verses above?

    _____

    _____

    b. According to Hebrews 11:1–6, what was it about the men of old, Abel, and Enoch that made them pleasing to God?

    _____

    _____

    c. How can you and I be pleasing to God?

    _____

    _____

    Faith is not a static concept in the mind but an active living out of God's word. To have faith in God is to act; it is to obey him willingly from the heart.

    d. In spite of the fact that you believe in God, do you sometimes find that in your deepest heart of hearts you don't believe he will answer you when you pray and therefore you don't expect him to answer you?

    _____

    _____

    James says, "If any of you lacks wisdom, let him ask of God, who gives to all generously and without reproach, and it will be given to him. *But he must ask in faith without any doubting,* for the one who doubts is like the surf of the sea, driven and tossed by the wind. For *that man ought not to expect that he will receive anything from the Lord,* being a double-minded man, unstable in all his ways" (James 1:5–8, emphasis added).

e. According to these verses in James, in one word, what is the characteristic that will hinder effective praying?

_____

f. In your mind, travel back to your most recent prayer. Being as honest and objective as possible, analyze the "faith quotient" (size, quantity, strength, and quality of your faith in God) evidenced in that prayer. On a scale from one to ten, where do you believe your faith quotient falls, #1 being the least faith in God and #10 being the greatest?

Doubt   Faith

□---1--------2--------3--------4--------5--------6--------7--------8--------9--------10---□

g. Were you at #10, sitting on the solid rock of Hebrews 11:6? Or #1, floundering in the surf of doubt like the man in James 1:6? Or were you somewhere in between?

_____

_____

h. Is the faith quotient you marked on the line above the norm for you? Or do you typically have more or less faith that God exists and that he rewards those who diligently seek him?

_____

_____

i. If your norm is different from what you checked for your most recent prayer, mark your norm on the numbered scale above under point "f."

Day 2
Faith Grows

All of us need to grow in our faith in God. But what makes our faith grow?

1. Read Matthew 10:1; 17:14–21 and Mark 9:14–24.

The passages in Matthew 17 and Mark 9 record the same incident of the father who brought his demon-possessed boy to the disciples for healing. But the disciples could not cast out the demon, even though Jesus had given them authority to do so. Though we can learn a number of things from these verses, I want to focus on just two:

a. Jesus' response to the faith of the disciples, and

b. Jesus' response to the faith of the boy's father.

The disciples lived with Jesus every day for three years, saw him do many astounding, miraculous works, and heard him teach. Jesus had also commissioned them to preach and duplicate the miracles he did. Yet they still needed to grow in faith. Matthew 17:19–20 reads:

> Then the disciples came to Jesus privately and said, "Why could we not drive it out?" And He said to them, "Because of the littleness of your faith; for truly I say to you, if you have faith the size of a mustard seed, you will say to this mountain, 'Move from here to there,' and it will move; and nothing will be impossible to you."

c. The disciples knew God wanted them to cast out the demon, didn't they? They hadn't forgotten Jesus gave them the power (authority) to cast it out, had they? (Matthew 10:1; 17:17)

_____

d. To what did Jesus attribute their failure to cast out the demon? (Matthew 17:20)

_____

Their faith was not of the quality to meet this difficult challenge. It was too little or imperfect,[4] mixed with doubt and unbelief (Matthew 17:20; 21:21–22; Mark 9:19). As a result, they were ineffective. Jesus' remedy was not bigger faith but rather exercising the faith they had, even faith the size of a tiny mustard seed— small but alive and growing. It produces great results in comparison to its size.

Jesus gave further insight to the process of healing in this particular case. He said to them, "This kind cannot come out by anything but prayer" (Mark 9:29) and "This kind does not go out except by prayer and fasting" (Matthew 17:21). Obviously, in dealing with supernatural powers of darkness (such as demonic beings), we need to be sensitive to spiritual dynamics. Here the disciples learned that they still had to call on God to intervene (prayer and fasting) even though they had authority to cast out demons and heal. The boy's healing and deliverance depended on it.

2. Read Luke 10:17–22.

    a. What was the disciples' joy *not* to be focused on? (v. 20)

    _____

    b. Who was to be the focus of their joy and, therefore, their faith? (v. 22)

    _____

The disciples needed to learn to focus not on the situation or the gifts Jesus gave them for serving him (the ability to cast out demons and heal), but on the giver of those gifts: Jesus himself. Likewise, our faith must never be in our ability or the gifts God gives for serving him. Our faith must be in the one who gives us the ability and gifts to do God's work, God himself, through Jesus Christ the Son. You don't need mountain-size faith to move mountains. You only need to exercise mustard-seed-size faith in the God who made mountains.

Day 3
Faith Persists

Mustard-seed faith, rooted in the person of God, acts. It is not uncertain or cowardly in the face of daunting circumstances, for its focus is God. Consequently, mustard-seed faith will not be intimidated or stopped by circumstances that are overwhelming from a human standpoint. It will perform feats exponentially greater than itself. But what about when we do have doubt mixed with our faith when we come to God in prayer? Is there any hope God will answer our prayers?

1. Read Mark 9:20–24 (NIV), quoted here:

> [20]So they brought him. When the spirit saw Jesus, it immediately threw the boy into a convulsion. He fell to the ground and rolled around, foaming at the mouth.
> [21]Jesus asked the boy's father, "How long has he been like this?"
> "From childhood," he answered.[22] "It has often thrown him into fire or water to kill him. But if you can do anything, take pity on us and help us."
> [23]"'If you can'?" said Jesus. "Everything is possible for one who believes."
> [24]Immediately the boy's father exclaimed, "I do believe; help me overcome my unbelief!"

Mark records the same incident of the demon-possessed boy from whom the disciples could not cast out the demon. But he adds a significant exchange between the father of the boy and Jesus. The father's cry, "If you can do anything," reveals his hope and hesitation, his faith and fear, his desire and doubt about Jesus' ability to do what his disciples could not do. Can you relate to the father's faith, buffeted as it was by doubt?

a. What did Jesus say in verse 23?

_____

b. What was the father's response to Jesus? (v. 24)

_____

c. This cry of the father, "I do believe; help me overcome my unbelief," has been called the Doubter's Prayer[5]. Have you ever prayed this prayer?

_____

d. According to Mark 9:25–27, what was Jesus' response to the father's prayer?

_____

e. What does Jesus' action of healing the boy reveal about the character of God? (See also Exodus 34:5–8 and Psalm 103:13–14.)

_____

f. What can we learn from the doubter's prayer about how to deal with doubt and unbelief?

_____

g. What can we expect from the Lord in response to our own doubter's prayer?

_____

h. What, or rather who, was the object of the doubting father's faith? (Mark 9:22)

_____

i. Who should be the object of our faith as well?

_____

God *expects* us to have faith in him. "He who comes to God must believe that He is" (Hebrews 11:6). This is an absolute given.

Yet God "has compassion on those who fear Him. For He Himself knows our frame; He is mindful that we are but dust" (Psalm 103:13–14). He recognizes the faith we do have and helps us overcome our doubt and lack of faith when we cry out to him. He compassionately answers our prayers of desperate faith. He expects us then to move closer to mustard-seed faith.

j. Do you suspect the father of the healed boy moved from doubting faith in Jesus to mustard-seed faith? Would you have done so?

_____

k. If you are wrestling with doubt as you pray, will you make the choice to turn from doubt to active faith in God, just as the boy's father did?

_____

Jesus made it clear that the goal is to move toward a growing, active faith. Faith the size of a mustard seed, rooted in God, produces results greater than itself. This is the faith that pleases God.

Day 4
Moving from Faith to Faith

So how exactly can we move toward mustard-seed faith, faith that is alive and growing, faith that pleases God?

1. Read Genesis 12:1–5 and Hebrews chapter 11.

a. Consider how Abraham and Sarah evidenced mustard-seed faith (Genesis 12:4–5; Hebrews 11:8–12). Write down your observations about their actions in response to God's command. What did they *do* by faith?

_____

_____

b. What was Sarah's mind-set that enabled her to act in faith? What should be our mind-set? (Hebrews 11:11)

_____

_____

c. What challenges to your faith have you experienced? Name at least one, or your current challenge.

_____

_____

d. How did you evidence (or how are you now evidencing) mustard-seed faith in that circumstance?

_____

_____

e. If you did not/do not have mustard-seed faith in your circumstance, what might it look like if you did? What "mountains" would have to move?

_____

_____

f. In light of what you learned about Abraham and Sarah's faith in God, consider your faith quotient (see question 1.g. under Day 1). What steps might you need to take to move toward a mustard-seed faith that is rooted in the character of God, faith that considers him faithful to his word, which earnestly and diligently seeks God … the kind of faith that pleases God?

_____

_____

_____

_____

_____

_____

2. Read Hebrews 12:1–2, quoted here (emphasis added):

> Therefore, since we have so great a cloud of witnesses surrounding us, let us also lay aside every encumbrance and the sin which so easily entangles us, and let us run with endurance the race that is set before us, *fixing our eyes on Jesus, the author and perfecter of faith*, who for the joy set before Him endured the cross, despising the shame, and has sat down at the right hand of the throne of God.

a. Circle the three things we are *to do* in the verses above, and list them below:
   - Let us _____
   - Let us _____
   - Fixing our eyes _____

b. In your own words, list the three things we are to do, according to these verses, to help us grow in faith:

_____

_____

c. Compare Hebrews 12:1–2 with Paul's verses about "forgetting what lies behind and reaching forward to what lies ahead, I press on toward the goal for the prize of the upward call of God in Christ Jesus" (Philippians 3:13–14). Note the similarities.

_____

_____

One of the significant ways in which we grow toward a mustard-seed faith that moves mountains is to keep our focus on Jesus, observing and imitating him. He is the one who set the perfect example of living by faith. We observe Jesus by reading his Word; we imitate him by living out God's truths as he did, in complete abandonment and loving obedience to his Father (Hebrews 12:2).

d. We also grow in faith, live by faith, and pray in faith by learning from:
   • those who walked by faith in the past (the cloud of witnesses), and
   • those who are walking by faith today.

e. How might we learn from those who lived before us?

_____

_____

f. How can we learn from those among us today who have a growing faith and walk with the Lord?

_____

_____

g. Consider these ways to learn from one another:
   • spending time in the Scriptures reading about those who walked with God,
   • reading books written by godly men and women of the past and present, and
   • spending time with men and women of God who are presently living out their belief in God.

h. Can you think of other ways we can learn from one another?

_____

_____

Paul said we should pattern our lives after these people, following their example of faith and obedience as they follow Jesus (Philippians 3:17).

What is one thing God taught you through this lesson?

_____

What Scripture especially spoke to you?

_____

What are you going to do in obedience to what God taught you?

_____

List the action steps you must take to be obedient to God. (The first step may be to go to a fellow believer who is already doing what God has spoken to you about.)

_____

_____

_____

Consider committing to the action steps below to help you move closer to being a person who seeks God diligently, believing that he will hear and reward your prayers of faith. Even to moving mountains.

Resolve to:

a. Focus my eyes on Jesus Christ, spending time with him in his Word, studying his life and teachings as well as the other Scriptures. Put the teachings of Scripture into practice, learning to live by faith (Ephesians 1:16–23; 3:14–21; 4:1–8, 9–13, 14–16; 5:1).

b. Spend time with men and women of God from the past by reading Scripture about them or reading books by or about them (Philippians 3:12–17).

c. Spend time with men and women of God who are alive today, following their example of mustard-seed faith as they follow Christ (Philippians 3:17). You can do this informally or in a small-group setting, and in serving together.

d. Pray with mustard-seed faith, confident in the character and promises of God (Matthew 21:21; Mark 11:23, 24; John 14:10–11, 12–15, 16–17, 21, 23–24; 1 Corinthians 13:2b).

e. Be caught living by faith (2 Peter 1:3–11; 3:18).

_____ (Initial here)

"[Enoch] obtained the witness that before his being taken up he was pleasing to God. And without faith it is impossible to please Him, for he who comes to God must believe that He is and that He is a rewarder of those who seek Him."

(Hebrews 11:5–6)

Lesson 8

Keep the Faith and Carry On

Day 1
Never Give Up

Read: *Brokenness to Beauty*, Part 4—Prayer

Chapter 15, Striking Back
Chapter 16, Persistent Prayer
Read Ephesians 6:10-18 every day this week. Choose at least one verse and memorize it.

> We must never give up on our problems or situations. ... We persist.
> That persistence in itself reveals our faith in God and honors him.
> (*Brokenness to Beauty*, 100)

Here is a definition of *persist* from Merriam-Webster Dictionary online:[6]
To go on resolutely or stubbornly in spite of opposition, importunity, or warning.
Synonym: *persevere*

Respond:

1. Read Luke 11:1–13; Matthew 15:21–28.

In Luke 11 we have the well-known "Ask, seek, knock" passage, which speaks to the fact that persistence in prayer will be rewarded with response from our good heavenly Father (Luke 11:9, 10, 13; Matthew 7:7–11).

In Matthew 15:21–28 we observe the Gentile woman's persistence in getting Jesus' attention (v. 23), even though she encountered resistance. When Jesus commends the woman for her "great faith," resulting in Jesus answering her plea to heal her daughter, it is clear that her faith in Jesus motivated her persistence in seeking help from him (v. 28).

2. Read Luke 18:1–8, quoted here:

> ¹Now He was telling them a parable to show that at all times they ought to pray and not to lose heart, ²saying, "In a certain city there was a judge who did not fear God and did not respect man. ³There was a widow in that city, and she kept coming to him, saying, 'Give me legal protection from my opponent.' ⁴For a while he was unwilling; but afterward he said to himself, 'Even though I do not fear God nor respect man, ⁵yet because this widow bothers me, I will give her legal protection, otherwise by continually coming she will wear me out.'" ⁶And the Lord said, "Hear what the unrighteous judge said; ⁷now, will not God bring about justice for His elect who cry to Him day and night, and will He delay long over them? ⁸I tell you that He will bring about justice for them quickly. However, when the Son of Man comes, will He find faith on the earth?"⁷

It seems appropriate to begin an investigation into persistent prayer by considering what Jesus taught about it. Luke records two parables that Jesus told to illustrate our need to persist or persevere in prayer. Our focus in this lesson will be on what Jesus taught in Luke 18.

In the first verse of Luke 18 we are given the reason Jesus told this parable: "to show that at all times they ought to pray and not to lose heart." He ends the parable by questioning if anyone will have faith "when the Son of Man comes," giving us a clue that persistent prayer (prayer that doesn't lose heart) is connected to faith (Luke 18:1, 8).⁸

a. What did Jesus teach through this parable? (See 18:1.)

_____

b. Why do you suppose Jesus told a parable to teach about praying and not losing heart? Would this parable be relevant and important to you? If so, how is it important to you?

_____

_____

c. List the two main characters named in this parable (18:2–3).

_____

3. Read Exodus 34:6–7, Psalm 55:22; 68:5–6; Psalm 103, and Jeremiah 9:23–24.

Contrast God with the judge. List what we know about the judge on the left-side column below, beneath "Traits of the Judge," using Luke 18:2, 4, 5.

On the right-side column, list what we know about God based on the Scriptures in #3 above. (Refer also to the list of what you learned about God from Psalm 145 in Lesson 1.)

Traits of the Judge	Traits of God
_____	_____
_____	_____
_____	_____
_____	_____

a. In contrast to the uncaring, unjust judge, what is God like (his character) as revealed in the verses in Exodus 34:6–7, Psalm 55:22; 68:5–6; Psalm 103, and Jeremiah 9:23–24?

_____

b. Based on the character of God revealed in these verses, would you say he cares about people?

_____

c. What do these verses reveal about how God cares for you if you are one of the "people of God" through faith in Jesus Christ?

_____

_____

God is gracious, just, and merciful. He cares about us, provides for us, and answers more of our prayers than we could ever keep track of.

But there are times when it seems he is slow to answer. When that happens, we need a shift in perspective from our view to God's view.

4. Compare the actions of the widow in the parable with those of the elect of God (Luke 18:3, 7).

    a. What did the widow do?   What do the elect/people of God do?
       _____   _____

    b. In a word or phrase, write the character trait they both exhibited by their actions.
       _____

    c. What is the character trait that Jesus zeroed in on as an example for us to exhibit in prayer? (See Luke 18:1, 5, 7.)
       _____

    d. What reason does Jesus give us to keep on praying and not lose heart? (See 18:7, 8.)
       _____
       _____

    e. Are you praying and not giving up? What are you doing that demonstrates your faith that God hears and will answer your prayers?
       _____
       _____

    f. If you've become discouraged, what will you do to change that so you will "pray and not lose heart"?
       _____

    g. How would recounting the mighty acts of the Lord help you "pray and not lose heart"? (Read Psalm 103 and 104.)
       _____

Day 2
Adjusting Our Timepieces

The question in Luke 18:7 "Will He delay long over them?" is also translated "Will he keep putting them off?" (NIV) and "Though he bear long with them" (KJV). This phrase, as well as many other Scriptures, speaks to God's patience toward mankind.

Aren't we glad he is that way when his patience is directed toward us? What about when he directs his patience toward those who are not good?

1. Read Matthew 5:44–45, quoted below (emphasis added):

    > I say to you, love your enemies and pray for those who persecute you, so that you may be sons of your Father who is in heaven; for *He causes His sun to rise on the evil and the good, and sends rain on the righteous and the unrighteous.*

    a. With whom is God kind and patient?

    _____

    b. Are you thankful God is kind and patient with you?

    _____

    c. Are you thankful God is kind and patient with the evil and unrighteous too?

    _____

    d. Why do you suppose he is kind and patient with them?

    _____

2. Read Jeremiah 9:24, John 3:15–17, Romans 10:6–17, Ephesians 2:1–5, 1 Timothy 2:1–6, and 2 Peter 3:8–9.

3. For each of the Scripture passages that follow, look for what we can learn

    a. about God,
    b. about ourselves, and
    c. about God's dealings with mankind and the reason for his patience with people in the world, both the good and the bad (righteous and unrighteous people).

Jeremiah 9:24

_____

John 3:15–17

_____

Romans 10:6–17

_____

Ephesians 2:1–5

_____

1 Timothy 2:1–6

_____

2 Peter 3:8–9

_____

The Scriptures above, and your own experience (revisit Lesson 1), reveal the compassion and the longsuffering of God. These are only a few examples of God's loving patience with mankind, both the people of God and those who don't know him.

4. Take a moment to praise and thank God for his goodness, kindness, compassion, and patience toward us all. Write your praise here:

    _____

    _____

    _____

    a. Now pray for your enemies and others who are without God, the ungodly, that they would repent and come to faith in Jesus Christ.

        _____

        _____

        _____

5. Read Isaiah 55:6–9, quoted below (emphasis added). Consider the apparent slowness of God at times to answer our prayers in light of these words.

    > ⁶Seek the Lord while He may be found; call upon Him while He is near. ⁷Let the wicked forsake his way and the unrighteous man his thoughts; and let him return to the Lord, and He will have compassion on him, and to our God, for He will abundantly pardon. ⁸*"For My thoughts are not your thoughts, nor are your ways My ways," declares the Lord. ⁹"For as the heavens are higher than the earth, so are My ways higher than your ways and My thoughts than your thoughts."*

    a. What is God willing to do for those who come to him in repentance? (See vv. 6–7.)

        _____

    b. According to Isaiah, why should we seek the Lord in humility? (See vv. 8–9.)

        _____

God "is and always will be God—holy—'other' than us. He is Creator; we are his creation. We must always approach him in humility and reverential fear." Therefore, "in prayer we seek his mind, his will, for how to pray about things and people. ... Prayer is ... about finding out what God wants to accomplish."[9]

We will always need a change of perspective when we come to prayer. We must look up to God's higher thoughts and ways, humbly submitting to his will for how to pray. Then we can pray with confidence and in the authority of Jesus' name.

Day 3
The Heart of the Matter

1. Read John 15:7, quoted here:

   If you abide in Me, and My words abide in you, ask whatever you wish, and it will be done for you.

   a. What is the prerequisite for asking and receiving whatever we wish from God?

   _____

2. Read John 15:10, quoted here (emphasis added):

   If you keep My commandments, you will abide in My love; just as I have kept My Father's commandments and abide in His love.

   a. How do we abide in Jesus' love?

   _____

   James said it another way:

   > [21]Therefore, putting aside all filthiness and all that remains of wickedness, in humility receive the word implanted, which is able to save your souls. [22]But prove yourselves *doers of the word*, and not merely hearers who delude themselves. [23]For if anyone is a hearer of the word and not a doer, he is like a man who looks at his natural face in a mirror; [24]for once he has looked at himself and gone away, he has immediately forgotten what kind of person he was. [25]*But one who looks intently at the perfect law, the law of liberty, and abides by it, not having become a forgetful hearer but an effectual doer, this man will be blessed in what he does.* (James 1:21–25, emphasis added)

    b. What does James say we are to do when we hear the Word of God? (See v. 22.)

_____

    c. What will bring blessing to what we do? (See v. 25.)

_____

The heart of the matter is simply what Jesus said: "If you love Me, you will keep My commandments" (John 14:15).

The Psalmist put it this way: "Delight yourself in the Lord; and He will give you the desires of your heart" (Psalm 37:4). If we love Jesus, we will delight in him and desire to do what he says. Obedience to God is rooted in love for him.

The widow in the parable in Luke 18 knew the law. This knowledge motivated her to be unceasing in her pursuit of justice.

1. According to Jesus (John 14:15; 15:7, 10), James (1:21–15), and the psalmist (Psalm 37:4), what do we need to *know* and *do* to persist and persevere in prayer, not giving up?

_____

When we love God and are living in obedience to his Word, pursuing his will and not our selfish ends, we too will be motivated to persist in faith-filled prayer. We will be certain that God will "bring justice to bear" for us, even if it is a long time in coming.

2. When it seems God is slow to answer your prayers, what truth do you need to remember? (See 2 Peter 3:8–9.)

_____

Let us, therefore, be patient, waiting in hope on our good and compassionate God to answer our prayers at the right time, humbly recognizing that "his understanding no one can fathom" (Isaiah 40:28 NIV).

Day 4
The Rest Is Up To You

1. So we come to the crux of the teaching of the parable. Regardless of the fact that God will answer prayer and bring justice to his people who cry out to him

unceasingly, Jesus wonders aloud, "When the Son of Man comes, will He find faith on the earth?" (Luke 18:8).

a. Will he find in you the firm belief, evidenced by your prayers, that God will answer you?

b. Will he find that you have such faith in God that you persist and persevere in seeking justice, not giving up in the face of opposition, injustice, and ungodliness?

c. In contrast to the widow who was not sure she'd ever get justice from an unrighteous judge, what can we be absolutely certain about when we pray to our heavenly Father? Give Scripture references.

d. What must you do to ensure that you will persevere in faith in the Lord, even in the face of suffering, opposition, oppression, rejection, injustice, ungodliness, or long waiting until the Lord brings justice to bear for you?

God has promised he will bring justice and he will answer prayer. Our confident hope is in the character of God and his faithful word.

Teach me Your way, O Lord, and lead me in a level path because of my foes. ... I would have despaired unless I had believed that I would see the goodness of the Lord in the land of the living. Wait for the Lord; be strong and let your heart take courage; yes, wait for the Lord. (Psalm 27:11, 13–14)

What did the Lord teach you from this lesson?

What will you do to obey the Lord in what you learned?

Lesson 6 opened with the statement "Prayer is something every Christian is supposed to know about and practice. And yet, many Christians feel inadequate when it comes to praying. Describe your feelings about prayer."

1. Summarize here what you wrote to describe your feelings about prayer. (Refer to lesson 6.)

   _____

   _____

   _____

2. After going through lessons 6, 7, and 8 on prayer, how have your feelings about prayer changed? What will you do differently in relation to prayer?

   _____

   _____

   _____

Resolve to:

1. Abide in Jesus' love by reading and obeying his Word so that God's desires will shape my prayers (Ephesians 6:18; 1 Thessalonians 4:1–7; 2 Peter 3:8–18; 1 John 3:10–24).
2. Confidently wait for and hope in the Lord, knowing he will answer prayer at the right time (Psalm 147:10–11; Isaiah 40:28–31; Matthew 7:7–12; Luke 11:5–13).

_____ (Initial here)

"Rejoice always and delight in your faith; be unceasing and persistent in prayer; in every situation [no matter what the circumstances] be thankful and continually give thanks to God; for this is the will of God for you in Christ Jesus."
(1 Thessalonians 5:16–18 AMP)

"Do not let this one fact escape your notice, beloved, that with the Lord one day is like a thousand years, and a thousand years like one day. The Lord is not slow about His promise, as some count slowness, but is patient toward you, not wishing for any to perish but for all to come to repentance."
(2 Peter 3:8–9)

Lesson 9

The Fragrance of Unity

Day 1
Foundation of Community

Read: *Brokenness to Beauty,* Part 4—Community

Chapter 17, A Community of Support
Chapter 18, Finding Community
Chapter 19, Support Groups
Chapter 20 The Gratitude Ingredient
Read Philippians 2:1–2 every day this week. Choose at least one verse and memorize it.

> When we go through rough times, being surrounded by loving, understanding, and helpful people, whether family or friends, is tremendously important in making it through intact. We cannot do this alone. ... Family, community, and church have all come into being by the orchestration of God, who made us to need and love each other. (*Brokenness to Beauty,* 108)

Respond:

Here are two definitions of *community* from *Oxford Dictionaries* online:[10]

1. A group of people living in the same place or having a particular characteristic in common.
2. A feeling of fellowship with others, as a result of sharing common attitudes, interests, and goals.

1. Read Genesis 1:26–28; 2:18, 21–24.

    a. Who comprised the first human community? (See 1:27; 2:18, 22–24.)

    _____

    b. What was God's first command to Adam and Eve? (See 1:28.)

    _____

The first human community consisted of Adam and Eve, husband and wife. These two were to expand community by bearing children, raising a family, and growing a society of people.

2. Read Psalm 133, quoted here:

    Behold, how good and how pleasant it is
    For brothers to dwell together in unity!
    It is like the precious oil upon the head,
    Coming down upon the beard,
    Even Aaron's beard,
    Coming down upon the edge of his robes.
    It is like the dew of Hermon
    Coming down upon the mountains of Zion;
    For there the Lord commanded the blessing—life forever.

Unity makes us "smell" good to those around us and to God. Unity is healing and life giving.

Throughout Scripture, both Old and New Testaments, God emphasizes healthy, loving human relationships. He desires us to live in harmony and peace, and he gave us his commandments to show us what that looks like and how to do it. The foundation of community is unity, in love.

The church, the people of God, is to be known for love, unity, and peace (John 17:20-21).

3. Read Matthew 5:9, John 13:35; 17:20–21, Ephesians 4:3, and Philippians 2:1–2.

Record what each verse or passage of Scripture teaches us about what the church, made up of individual followers of Jesus Christ, is to *be* and/or *do*.

a. Matthew 5:9 (See also Matthew 5:43–48; 1 Peter 1:14–16)

_____

b. John 13:35

_____

c. John 17:20–21

_____

d. Ephesians 4:3

_____

e. Philippians 2:1–2

_____

f. What other Scriptures can you think of that teach us the same things?

_____

Jesus instituted the church as the community of God's people and we benefit from it. We are made in the image of the triune God, the original community—Father, Son, and Holy Spirit—who live in perfect love and unity with one another. We, therefore, made in God's image, are social beings. We need one another; we are meant to live in unity. Since God is love (1 John 4:8), it should be no surprise that Jesus commanded his followers to "love one another." This love is a distinguishing mark of the church (John 13:35).

Day 2
Community Expressed through Hands and Feet

In Bible times, people had daily face-to-face relationships, as they do in many traditional cultures today. People saw and interacted with one another more frequently than we typically do in our present-day Western culture. We must work harder today to create community, that "feeling of fellowship with others, as a result of shared common attitudes, interests, and goals." Even in the church, it is worth the effort. This is why many churches encourage their members to meet in small groups, where face-to-face, first-name-basis relationships can form and grow, and where serving together and serving one another can take place naturally.[11]

We need one another, and never more so than when we are going through difficult times in our lives. Do you have a community of support? It is imperative that we work to make or find a community of people who are learning to love and care for one another.

Read the Scriptures listed below. Observe their examples of community and consider what is meant by "a community of support" based on what you discover. Describe the types of support you can identify in each passage and discuss (if you are in a group study) ways of developing or increasing similar dynamics in your own group.

1. Mark 2:1–5

    a. In what ways did members of this community express their love and support of one another?

    _____

    b. What assumptions can you make about how the four men felt about their paralyzed friend?

    _____

    c. Have you personally witnessed this level of supportive community action on behalf of another, in either your current group or another one?

    _____

    d. What do you think would need to happen, what would it take, to form community like that?

    _____

2. Acts 9:36–42

    a. What kind of woman was Dorcas? (See vv. 36, 39.)

    _____

    b. How did the widows express their love for Dorcas? (See vv. 37, 39.)

    _____

    c. Was this community of disciples comprised only of widows? Who are the others mentioned? (See vv. 38–39.)

    _____

d. Who went to get Peter and how did they express their esteem and concern for Dorcas? (See v. 38.)

_____

e. Does your community of support have both men and women disciples of Jesus who care for and help one another in ways similar to those in Dorcas's group? Describe the ways members of your community of support have helped others within the group or outside of it.

_____

_____

3. Acts 4:23–31

The events in Acts 4:23–31 took place following the release of Peter and John from prison after their arrest for healing the lame man in the temple, recorded in Acts 3. The Sanhedrin, the high court of the Jewish people, demanded they stop preaching in Jesus' name, but Peter and John refused to stop preaching.

a. Do you belong to a community of believers who prays for one another the way Peter and John's church prayed?

_____

b. What did the disciples pray for? (See vv. 29–30.)

_____

c. Have you and your group prayed that way in the face of difficulties?

_____

d. Does your community of support have the same knowledge of the Word of God and heart for speaking forth the gospel with boldness that Peter and John's group had?

_____

e. What difference can love for God and his Word make in the dynamics of a group of people?

_____

f. How can you help foster or maintain such love for God and his Word in your group?

_____

4. Acts 4:32–35

    a. How was this congregation of believers demonstrating their faith in the God of the Bible and living out Jesus' command to love one another? (See vv. 32, 34–35.)

    _____

    _____

    b. Three significant things came about because of the compassionate actions of the congregation toward one another as they lived out their faith in obedience to Jesus. What are they? (See vv. 33–34a.)

    _____

    _____

    c. Would you characterize your church or small group as one that lives out Jesus' command to love one another in ways similar to those of the church in Acts?

    _____

    _____

    d. In what practical ways do those in your church or group express love for one another?

    _____

    _____

    e. Have you experienced the love of God through members of your community of support? If so, describe the ways.

    _____

    _____

    f. Have you expressed the love of Jesus to others in your group in ways similar to the early church in Acts? What did that look like?

    _____

    _____

Day 3
Community Expressed Through Heads and Hearts

1. Read James 5:13–20.

    We typically read these verses in connection with faith, prayer, and healing.

However, read the whole passage from the perspective of community and note what you see about it; consider the ways we should relate to and serve one another.

a. Does it appear that the people James addressed knew one another fairly well? Which verse or verses influenced you to make that decision?

    _____

b. Do you think James assumed these believers met together regularly? How can we know? (Hint: The phrase "is anyone among you" is repeated three times in verses 13 and 14, and "if any among you" once in verse 19.)

    _____

c. Below is a list of three categories of life situations taken from verses 13–16. What does James instruct us to do when we find ourselves in these situations? (See vv. 13–14.)
    *   Is anyone among you suffering? _____
    *   Is anyone cheerful? _____
    *   Is any among you sick? _____

d. What are we instructed to do that would affect the physical and spiritual health of the church members in a positive way? (See v. 16.)

    _____

e. In verses 14 and 15 the elders of the church are called upon to pray in faith for the sick. Who are the others tasked with responsibilities to the sick? (See v. 16.)

    _____

f. What are the two things James tells these people to do that will affect the sick person? (See v. 16.)

    _____

g. Circle any words listed below that would describe attitudes and attributes needed in believers' relationships with one another in order to successfully "confess your sins to one to another, and pray for one another so that you may be healed."
    Accountability, vulnerability, a college degree, humility, graciousness, forgiveness, new car, forbearance, big house, patience, lovingkindness, personal make-over, trust, transparency, reconciliation, latest clothes fashions, faith, gentleness, all "A's" kids, love

    h. Note any other words you think are descriptive of attitudes and attributes we must have to be the kind of community of believers in Jesus Christ who would look like the people James instructed us to be.

_____

    i.   Are you part of such a community? Does your community of support have this level of trust and accountability as well as the other character traits seen in James 5 and described above?

_____

    j.   What can you do to start to develop or maintain this in your small group or church?

_____

2. Read Galatians 6:1–5, 7–10.

Paul wrote the book of Galatians to all the Christians in the region of Galatia, who likely met in small groups. Read it in that context, as though addressed to your local church or small group.

    a. What does it mean to be "caught in any trespass"? (See v. 1.)

_____

    b. How would you describe a "spiritual" person? (See v. 1.) What Bible verses can you use to support your idea? (Read Galatians 5:14, 16–17, 22–25.)

_____

    c. What would be the opposite of a "spiritual" person? (Read 1 Corinthians 3:1–3; Galatians 5:15, 19–21, 26)

_____

    d. Could any of us ever be in the place of the one who is "caught" in a transgression? (1 Corinthians 10:11–13; Galatians 6:1, 3)

_____

    e. What is our responsibility as a community of believers toward the one who falls because of a sin committed? (See vv. 1, 2.)

_____

f. What is the key word in this passage for the manner in which we restore a brother or sister? (See v. 1.)

g. Why is it especially important for us to use gentleness? (See Galatians 6:1c, 3, 5; Matthew 5:7; 7:1–5, 12.)

h. To whom are we finally accountable for our own actions? (See Galatians 6:5, 7.)

i. To what two groups of people are we, as a community of believers, to "do good"? (See v. 10.)

j. Is there ever a time to give up doing good to others? Why or why not? (See vv. 9–10.)

k. Is your community of support living up to Paul's admonition to believers in the book of Galatians?

l. How can you help make or keep your group such a community?

Day 4
A Life of Gratitude

When we experience the mercy and lovingkindness of God through others, our response should be one of gratitude and praise to God.

How many ways can you think of to show gratitude to God and others for their care?

Brokenness to Beauty Bible Study

1. Read Mark 1:29–31, quoted here:

> Immediately after they came out of the synagogue, they came into the house of Simon and Andrew, with James and John. Now Simon's mother-in-law was lying sick with a fever; and immediately they spoke to Jesus about her. And He came to her and raised her up, taking her by the hand, and the fever left her, and she waited on them.

Simon Peter's mother-in-law, possibly a widow, was in the home with her son-in-law and her daughter, Peter's wife. It is quite common even today, in traditional cultures around the world, for extended family members to live together in the home.

Usually the women cook, and clean, and serve the family and guests. Grandmas often show their love by plying folks with food. From this passage, we may surmise that Peter's mother-in-law was greatly loved, because those around her were quick to tell Jesus about the fever that had laid her low.

a. What three things did Jesus do in response to being told she was ill? (Look for the action words in verse 31.)

b. What was the result of Jesus' actions?

c. What did Peter's mother-in-law immediately do?

d. Do you think she began serving Jesus and the others in her home simply because work needed to be done? What do you think might have been her motive?

What a lesson for us! As soon as her feet hit the floor, she was taking care of her guests. She offered a sacrifice of thanksgiving to God by doing what she knew best to do: serve. And Jesus accepted her service.

e. When you have gone through difficult times and people came to your aid, how did you express gratitude to God and to them?

_____

2. Read Psalm 50:14–15, 23.

   a. From God's perspective, when we offer thanksgiving to him, what are we ultimately doing?

_____

3. Read Hebrews 13:15–16.

   a. How often should we give God praise, the "fruit of lips that give thanks to His name"? (See v. 15.)

_____

   b. When they received this letter, the Hebrew Christians were under threat of persecution for living out their faith in Jesus. Are you being persecuted for the sake of Jesus Christ?

_____

   c. Do you have a lifestyle of continually offering to God a sacrifice of praise whether you are in good times or bad? (Maybe you should ask your spouse, children, or a friend to answer this for you.)

_____

   d. Are you offering to God the sacrifices of "doing good and sharing" with others, in good times and in bad?

_____

We can express love for one another, as Jesus commanded his followers to do, in ways much like the examples seen in the Bible passages we studied in this lesson. Love looks like the sacrificial assistance and care given to others we should see, and often do see, within the church. This is what a community of support should be like. "Beyond all these things put on love, which is the perfect bond of unity" (Colossians 3:14).

Community in unity and love is what makes us "smell" good to God and to other people.

What did you learn from God's Word in this lesson?

_____

_____

_____

How will you put what you've learned into practice?

_____

_____

_____

Resolve to:

a. Live in peace, love, and unity with fellow Christians, and everyone else, as much as possible (John 17:22–23; Romans 12:9–21; 13:8; 14:19; Ephesians 4:1–3).

b. Strive to build and maintain, in cooperation with others, a community of support that looks like the examples in the Bible (John 13:13–17).

c. Make sacrificial thanksgiving my lifestyle, honoring God (Hebrews 13:15–16).

d. Joyfully please God by offering to him the sacrifice of "doing good and sharing" with others, living out true community (Acts 2:42–47; 4:32–35; 2 Corinthians 8 and 9; Galatians 6:2, 9–10).

e. Put into practice what I learned from this lesson, which is:

_____

_____

_____ (Initial here)

"About brotherly love: You don't need me to write you because
you yourselves are taught by God to love one another. In fact,
you are doing this toward all the brothers in the entire region. ...
But we encourage you, brothers, to do so even more."
(1 Thessalonians 4:9–10 HCSB)

Lesson 10

Hope Unseen to Hope Fulfilled

Day 1

On Purpose

Read: *Brokenness to Beauty*, Part 5—Purpose

Chapter 21, A Reason to Get Up in the Morning

Chapter 22, Choices

Chapter 23, Kingdom Big

Read 2 Corinthians 4:1–18; 5:1–12 every day this week. Choose at least one verse and memorize it.

> Even when I feel insignificant, ... I am comforted because I am part of something much greater than myself. ... I am part of God's purposes for his world. I can with confidence know there is meaning to my life. (*Brokenness to Beauty*, 131)

I love the following blog post quote by Debbie W. Wilson, author of *Give Yourself a Break: Discover the Secrets to God's Rest* and *Little Women, Big God: It's Not the Size of Your Problems but the Size of Your God*, included here with permission:[12]

> When someone recommends a book, I want to know if it has a good ending. Knowing it will end well helps me wade through the challenging parts of the story.

> Would it make a difference if you knew your pain had a purpose? …
> Would it help if you knew your story was going to have an amazing
> ending? …
> God uses trials to carve out in us the capacity to hold His ultimate
> gifts. "Therefore we do not lose heart. … For our light and momentary
> troubles are achieving for us an eternal weight of glory that far
> outweighs them all. So we fix our eyes not on what is seen, but on
> what is unseen. For what is seen is temporal, but what is unseen is
> eternal" (2 Corinthians 4:16–18 NIV).

This final lesson from the last section of the book, *Brokenness to Beauty*, is of utmost importance, for chapters 21–23 point us toward the answers to the deepest questions of our souls: *Why am I here? What is the purpose of my life?* It also points to God's answers to those questions.

We all need to find a purpose that is worth living for, a reason to get up in the morning. The something bigger than we are that is worthy of our wholehearted pursuit.

So what is God doing in the world? What are his purposes? Previously we said it is the redemption of mankind in a restored earth. It is that, but it is even more. From the Scriptures we learn that God has been steadily on the move throughout human history to take back his kingdom from the usurper, Satan. In fact, Jesus came "to destroy the works of the devil" (1 John 3:8). Our redemption, and that of the earth, is part of his plan as he resolutely moves toward establishing his eternal kingdom. God will sovereignly rule in righteousness, and we will serve and rule with him forever.[13] We have something worth getting up for in the morning!

Respond:

1. Read Romans 8:14–25, quoted here:

    > [14]All who are being led by the Spirit of God, these are sons of God.
    > [15]For you have not received a spirit of slavery leading to fear again,
    > but you have received a spirit of adoption as sons by which we cry
    > out, "Abba! Father!" [16]The Spirit Himself testifies with our spirit that
    > we are children of God, [17]and if children, heirs also, heirs of God and
    > fellow heirs with Christ, if indeed we suffer with Him so that we may
    > also be glorified with Him.
    > [18]For I consider that the sufferings of this present time are not worthy
    > to be compared with the glory that is to be revealed to us. [19]For the
    > anxious longing of the creation waits eagerly for the revealing of the

sons of God. ²⁰For the creation was subjected to futility, not willingly, but because of Him who subjected it, in hope ²¹that the creation itself also will be set free from its slavery to corruption into the freedom of the glory of the children of God. ²²For we know that the whole creation groans and suffers the pains of childbirth together until now. ²³And not only this, but also we ourselves, having the first fruits of the Spirit, even we ourselves groan within ourselves, waiting eagerly for our adoption as sons, the redemption of our body. ²⁴For in hope we have been saved, but hope that is seen is not hope; for who hopes for what he already sees? ²⁵But if we hope for what we do not see, with perseverance we wait eagerly for it.

a. Circle four names or titles used for followers of Jesus in Romans 8:14–17. (For example: v. 14—sons of God.)

_____

_____

_____

b. List at least five characteristics of followers of Jesus—things done *for* them or things they *do.* (See vv.14–17, 23, 25.)
(For example: v. 14—are led by the Spirit of God.)

_____

_____

_____

c. As followers of Jesus Christ, what are we looking forward to at the end of our earthly story? (See vv. 17, 23.)
V. 17: "may also be _____ with him."
V. 23: "for our adoption as sons, the redemption of _____ "

d. What is it that we endure now but which pales in comparison to the glory of God we will share with Jesus one day? (See vv. 17–18.)

_____

e. What else is waiting and groaning for the final redemption and glory of the children of God? (See vv. 19–22.)

_____

    f.   Circle the three important words that describe what we are to *possess* or *do* while we wait for our new bodies and future glory at our final adoption as sons of God. (See v. 25.)

_____

Scripture tells us the end of our earthly story and the beginning of our eternal story, and it is worth living for. Followers of Jesus Christ should know these truths from God's Word and gain hope from them.

We will have trials and suffering in this life, and though we have been freed from the power and penalty of sin now (Romans 6), one day we will also be set free from the *presence* of sin. We will have new, sin-free, undying bodies, like Jesus' body, at the culmination of our salvation when our redemption, our adoption as sons and daughters, is completed. All creation will be set free from sin's penalty: death. God is truly making all things new (2 Corinthians 5:17; Revelation 21:5).

    g.   What can we possess now, even in the midst of our sufferings, according to Romans 8:24–25?

_____

It is this hope of future glory with Jesus that enables us to persevere to the end, when we will be glorified with Jesus Christ for all eternity.

Day 2
A Bird's-Eye View of God's Purposes

Let's "helicopter" through the Bible to get the big picture of God's acts and purposes from the beginning. We will also see what men and women, the crown of God's creation, have been up to throughout human history. And we will discover what followers of Jesus Christ have to live for in the here and now, while living with the long view of eternity in our sight.

Read and respond to each group of verses below.

Our Story Begins
Note *who is acting* and *what is happening* verse by verse.

1.   Genesis 1:1, 26, 27, 31

    "¹In the beginning God created the heavens and the earth."

"²⁶Then God said, "Let Us make man in Our image, according to Our likeness. ...

_____

²⁷God created man in His own image, in the image of God He created him; male and female He created them."

_____

"³¹God saw all that He had made, and behold, it was very good. And there was evening and there was morning, the sixth day."

_____

2. Genesis 2:16–17

"The Lord God commanded the man, saying, "From any tree of the garden you may eat freely; but from the tree of the knowledge of good and evil you shall not eat, for in the day that you eat from it you will surely die."

a. What was the one thing God prohibited? What did God say was the consequence for disobedience?

_____

3. Genesis 3:4

"The serpent said to the woman, 'You surely will not die!'"
a. Who was the serpent directly opposing by his statement in verse 4?

_____

b. Was the serpent telling the truth when he declared that what God said was not true?

_____

c. How do we know who was lying, God or Satan? (Hint: Are the original Adam and Eve alive today?)

_____

4. Genesis 3:6

"When the woman saw that the tree was good for food, and that it was a delight to the eyes, and that the tree was desirable to make one wise, she took from its fruit and ate; and she gave also to her husband with her, and he ate."

    a. What did Adam and Eve do, in direct opposition to what God told them not to do, that changed human history? (Compare 1 John 2:15–17 with Genesis 3:6.)

    _____

5. Genesis 3:19

    "By the sweat of your face
    You will eat bread,
    Till you return to the ground,
    Because from it you were taken;
    For you are dust,
    And to dust you shall return."

    a. What was the ultimate result of Eve and Adam's acts (Genesis 3:6)?

    _____

    b. Was this death limited to only our bodies? (Ephesians 2:1–3)

    _____

6. Romans 5:12

    "Therefore, just as through one man sin entered into the world, and death through sin, and so death spread to all men, because all sinned ..."

    a. How many people were affected by death, the result of one man, Adam's sin?

    _____

Redemption Unfolds

When were God's works of creation and redemption completed? Note on the line below each verse.

1. Genesis 2:2–3

    "By the seventh day God completed His work which He had done, and He rested on the seventh day from all His work which He had done. Then God blessed the seventh day and sanctified it, because in it He rested from all His work which God had created and made."

    _____

2. Ephesians 1:4

    "He chose us in Him before the foundation of the world, that we would be holy and blameless before Him."

    _____

3. 1 Peter 1:18–20

    "You were not redeemed with perishable things ... but with precious blood, as of a lamb unblemished and spotless, the blood of Christ. For He was foreknown before the foundation of the world, but has appeared in these last times for the sake of you."

    _____

The first curse pronounced by God also contains a promise for mankind.

1. Genesis 3:13–15, AMP

    "¹³Then the Lord God said to the woman, 'What is this that you have done?' And the woman said, 'The serpent beguiled and deceived me, and I ate [from the forbidden tree].' ¹⁴The Lord God said to the serpent,

    'Because you have done this,
    You are cursed more than all the cattle,
    And more than any animal of the field;
    On your belly you shall go,
    And dust you shall eat
    All the days of your life.

    '¹⁵And I will put enmity (open hostility)
    Between you and the woman,
    And between your seed (offspring) and her Seed;
    He shall [fatally] bruise your head,
    And you shall [only] bruise His heel.'"

    a. What was cursed? Who was animating the serpent? What would he do to the Seed of the woman?

        _____

    b. Who is the Seed of the woman? What would he do to the serpent/Satan?

        _____

   c. What was the promise?[14]

What are some of God's intentions for his redeemed people? List on the lines beneath each verse.

1. John 13:34

"A new commandment I give to you, that you love one another, even as I have loved you, that you also love one another."

2. Titus 2:14

"Who gave Himself for us to redeem us from every lawless deed, and to purify for Himself a people for His own possession, zealous for good deeds."

3. Romans 8:29

"For those whom He foreknew, He also predestined to become conformed to the image of His Son, so that He would be the firstborn among many brethren."

4. Hebrews 12:1–14 (HCSB)

"[1]Therefore, since we also have such a large cloud of witnesses surrounding us, let us lay aside every weight and the sin that so easily ensnares us. Let us run with endurance the race that lies before us, [2]keeping our eyes on Jesus, the source and perfecter of our faith, who for the joy that lay before Him endured a cross and despised the shame and has sat down at the right hand of God's throne.

"[3]For consider Him who endured such hostility from sinners against Himself, so that you won't grow weary and lose heart. [4]In struggling against sin, you have not yet resisted to the point of shedding your blood. [5]And you have forgotten the exhortation that addresses you as sons:

"'My son, do not take the Lord's discipline lightly
or faint when you are reproved by Him,
[6]for the Lord disciplines the one He loves
and punishes every son He receives.'

"[7]Endure suffering as discipline: God is dealing with you as sons. For what son is there that a father does not discipline? [8]But if you are without discipline—which all receive—then you are illegitimate children and not sons. [9]Furthermore, we had natural fathers discipline us, and we respected them. Shouldn't we submit even more to the Father of spirits and live? [10]For they disciplined us for a short time based on what seemed good to them, but He does it for our benefit, so that we can share His holiness. [11]No discipline seems enjoyable at the time, but painful. Later on, however, it yields the fruit of peace and righteousness to those who have been trained by it.

"[12]Therefore strengthen your tired hands and weakened knees, [13]and make straight paths for your feet, so that what is lame may not be dislocated but healed instead.

"[14]Pursue peace with everyone, and holiness—without it no one will see the Lord."

---

a. How are we to view the suffering that comes into our lives? (See v. 7.)

---

b. What is the desired end-result of suffering—God's training for his children? (See vv. 11, 14.)

Day 3
The Face of Mercy

Going verse by verse, circle the character traits of God at work on our behalf (example: mercy). Then write them on the lines below the verses.

1. Ephesians 2:4–6

"God, being rich in mercy, because of His great love with which He loved us, even when we were dead in our transgressions, made us alive together with Christ (by grace you have been saved), and raised us up with Him, and seated us with Him in the heavenly places in Christ Jesus."

---

2. Ephesians 2:7–9 (AMP)

"[He did this] so that in the ages to come He might [clearly] show the immeasurable and unsurpassed riches of His grace in [His] kindness toward us in Christ Jesus [by providing for our redemption]. For it is by grace [God's remarkable compassion and favor drawing you to Christ] that you have been saved [actually delivered from judgment and given eternal life] through faith. And this [salvation] is not of yourselves [not through your own effort], but it is the [undeserved, gracious] gift of God; not as a result of [your] works [nor your attempts to keep the Law], so that no one will [be able to] boast or take credit in any way [for his salvation]."

Living in Light of Mercy and Grace

What are we to do in response to God's mercy, grace, and love? Rewrite in your own words.

1. Romans 12:1

   "Therefore I urge you, brethren, by the mercies of God, to present your bodies a living and holy sacrifice, acceptable to God, which is your spiritual service of worship."

2. Philippians 1:27

   "Only conduct yourselves in a manner worthy of the gospel of Christ … standing firm in one spirit, with one mind striving together for the faith of the gospel."

3. Ephesians 4:1–3

   "I, the prisoner of the Lord, implore you to walk in a manner worthy of the calling with which you have been called, with all humility and gentleness, with patience, showing tolerance for one another in love, being diligent to preserve the unity of the Spirit in the bond of peace."

Day 4

Jesus and the Kingdom of God

Going verse by verse through the passages below, in your own words describe in a short phrase or sentence what Jesus Christ *has done*, is *doing now*, or *will do* in God's kingdom.

1. Daniel 7:13–14 (see also vv. 9–12)

    "I kept looking in the night visions, and behold, with the clouds of heaven One like a Son of Man was coming, and He came up to the Ancient of Days and was presented before Him. And to Him was given dominion, glory and a kingdom, that all the peoples, nations and men of every language might serve Him. His dominion is an everlasting dominion which will not pass away; and His kingdom is one which will not be destroyed."

    _____

2. Philippians 2:10–11

    "At the name of Jesus every knee will bow, of those who are in heaven and on earth and under the earth, ¹¹and that every tongue will confess that Jesus Christ is Lord, to the glory of God the Father."

    _____

3. Colossians 1:16–18, 20

    "¹⁶For by Him all things were created, both in the heavens and on earth, visible and invisible, whether thrones or dominions or rulers or authorities—all things have been created through Him and for Him."

    _____

    "¹⁷He is before all things, and in Him all things hold together."

    _____

    "¹⁸He is also head of the body, the church; and He is the beginning, the firstborn from the dead, so that He Himself will come to have first place in everything."

    _____

"²⁰Through Him to reconcile all things to Himself, having made peace through the blood of His cross; through Him, I say, whether things on earth or things in heaven."

4. Revelation 21:3–5

"³I heard a loud voice from the throne, saying, 'Behold, the tabernacle of God is among men, and He will dwell among them, and they shall be His people, and God Himself will be among them.'"

"⁴He will wipe away every tear from their eyes; and there will no longer be any death; there will no longer be any mourning, or crying, or pain; the first things have passed away."

"⁵He who sits on the throne said, 'Behold, I am making all things new.'"

5. Revelation 22:12–13

"Behold, I am coming quickly, and My reward is with Me, to render to every man according to what he has done. I am the Alpha and the Omega, the first and the last, the beginning and the end."

You and the Kingdom of God

Verse by verse, record in your own words what these Scriptures teach us about our part and purpose in the present and future kingdom of God.

1. Galatians 6:9–10

"Let us not lose heart in doing good, for in due time we will reap if we do not grow weary. So then, while we have opportunity, let us do good to all people, and especially to those who are of the household of the faith."

2. 1 Peter 1:15–16

    "Like the Holy One who called you, be holy yourselves also in all your behavior; because it is written, 'You shall be holy, for I am holy.'"

    _____

3. 1 Peter 2:9

    "You are a chosen race, a royal priesthood, a holy nation, a people for God's own possession, so that you may proclaim the excellencies of Him who has called you out of darkness into His marvelous light."

    _____

4. 1 Peter 4:7

    "The end of all things is near; therefore, be of sound judgment and sober spirit for the purpose of prayer."

    _____

5. Matthew 28:18–20

    "Jesus came up and spoke to them, saying, 'All authority has been given to Me in heaven and on earth. Go therefore and make disciples of all the nations, baptizing them in the name of the Father and the Son and the Holy Spirit, teaching them to observe all that I commanded you; and lo, I am with you always, even to the end of the age.'"

    _____

6. Matthew 24:14

    "This gospel of the kingdom shall be preached in the whole world as a testimony to all the nations, and then the end will come."

    _____

7. Revelation 19:7–8

    "Let us rejoice and be glad and give the glory to Him, for the marriage of the Lamb has come and His bride has made herself ready.'" It was given to her to clothe herself in fine linen, bright and clean; for the fine linen is the righteous acts of the saints."

    _____

8. Revelation 22:3, 5

"³There will no longer be any curse; and the throne of God and of the Lamb will be in it, and His bond-servants will serve Him."

"⁵There will no longer be any night; and they will not have need of the light of a lamp nor the light of the sun, because the Lord God will illumine them; and they will reign forever and ever."

What an amazing revelation of God's purposes. And think of it, God calls us, individually and as the church—the community of God, the bride of Christ—to join him in working out his purposes! To that end, God is fitting us for that task today, especially through the trials that come into our lives.

Day 5
Getting Perspective

Let's summarize what we've seen in this helicopter ride through the Bible:

1. God created everything, including man and woman. And it was all very good. But we ruined it when, in Adam, we decided not to believe, trust, and obey God. Sin and death entered for all mankind. (See Genesis 1:1, 26–27, 31; 2:16–17; 3:4, 6, 19; Romans 5:12.)

2. God's plan to redeem mankind was complete before he finished creation. He rested on the seventh day because *all* his works were accomplished. (See Genesis 2:2–3; Ephesians 1:4; 1 Peter 1:18–20.)

3. Through Jesus Christ, and by faith in him, we can be redeemed, bought back by God to be his own. In Christ, we are made new, designed to live out his goodness and love through our actions. God shapes us into the image of Jesus Christ through our trials and suffering. (See John 13:34; Romans 8:29; Ephesians 2:10; Titus 2:14; Hebrews 12: 1–14.)

4. God fully revealed his mercy, grace, and love in Jesus Christ by all he did for us in his life, death and resurrection. We, the church, are living witnesses to the world and the universe of the love and mercy, grace and forgiveness, wisdom and power of God. (See Ephesians 2:4–9.)

5. In response to all God has done for us, we are to give our lives back to him and live worthy of him, in love for one another and forgiveness toward all men, proclaiming by word and deed the good news of the kingdom of God and salvation in Jesus Christ. (See Romans 12:1; Philippians 1:27; Ephesians 4:1.)

6. Jesus is fully God. He created everything by and for himself, has finished the work of salvation, is King over all kings and all authorities in heaven and on earth. He is the head of the church and will return to set up his eternal kingdom so that all the peoples, nations, and men of every language might serve him. He is coming back soon to judge all in righteousness, and he will live with us forever. (See Daniel 7:9–14; Philippians 2:10–11; Colossians 1:16–18, 20; Revelation 21:3–5; 22:12–13.)

7. We are called to be holy and to live in willing and loving obedience to God now, carrying the good news of the kingdom of God and salvation through Jesus Christ to those near and far who have not heard, doing good to all men. We will serve him and rule with him for all eternity in the new heaven and the new earth. (See Matthew 24:14; 28:18–20; Galatians 6:9–10; 1 Peter 1:15–16; 2:9; 4:7; Revelation 19:7–8; 22:3, 5.)

The Seven Wonders of the World are nothing compared to the eternal purposes of God! His purposes are so magnificent, so marvelous, we cannot do justice to them in a few paragraphs.

And these are only a few of the Scriptures that give us a glimpse of what God is about.

Let us make every effort to humbly seek out the treasures of God's Word in order to better understand and participate in his plans for the world, remembering that God's thoughts and ways are quite different from ours, much higher (Isaiah 55:6–9).

As we study the Word of God and are taught by the Spirit of God, we can begin to embrace his purposes for our lives. Then we will grasp the reason to get up one more day. Abiding with Jesus, obeying his word, we will find the hope that fixes our eyes on that which is beyond our present life and struggles, the hope of eternal life that will never disappoint us.

> Therefore, since we have been declared righteous by faith, we have peace with God through our Lord Jesus Christ. We have also obtained access through Him by faith into this grace in which we stand, and we rejoice in the hope of the glory of God. And not only that, but we also rejoice in our afflictions, because we know that affliction

produces endurance, endurance produces proven character, and proven character produces hope. This hope will not disappoint us, because God's love has been poured out in our hearts through the Holy Spirit who was given to us. (Romans 5:1–5 HCSB)

In God's Word we learn the end of the story and the meaning behind what we experience in this life. In God's Word we discover that the end of our earthly story is but the beginning of the fulfilment of our eternal hope, the hope of the glory of God.

As we grow in the knowledge of our Lord through reading his Word, and grow in grace as we put it into practice, walking and talking with God's Spirit every day, we can experience the grace and peace we long for in the midst of our suffering.
And we will come to know that all these things are wrapped up in the person of Jesus Christ. Much as the earth revolves around the sun, so our lives should revolve around Jesus Christ. When we grasp this truth, we join the faithful of past generations who looked expectantly to God, in whom their hope was anchored (Hebrews 12:1–3).

Now What?

In light of these truths about God's purposes for us and his world, we must ask, "How should we then live?"

You have been getting a glimpse of that answer as you worked your way through this Bible study. After each lesson you were asked, "What did you learn from this lesson?" and "What will you do about it?" Review your answers from each lesson and summarize what you learned and what you decided to do in obedience to God's prompting.

1)_____

2)_____

3)_____

4)_____

5)_____

6)_____

7)_____

8)_____

9)_____

You were also encouraged, in the "Resolve" sections, to make commitments based on the focus of each lesson. You initialed those promises, pledging to God to carry them out every day.

Review the promises you made in the "Resolve" section at the end of each of the previous nine lessons. Write them here:

1)_____
2)_____
3)_____
4)_____
5)_____
6)_____
7)_____
8)_____
9)_____

Notice the priority of the Word of God in these commitments. There is a reason for that. Through the Word of God and the work of his Spirit, you become "transformed by the renewing of your mind, so that you may prove what the will of God is, that which is good and acceptable and perfect" (Romans 12:2).

Take note also of the commitments to communicate with God in prayer, practice living in his presence daily, and praying in the spirit and according to the truth of God's Word, putting into practice what God teaches in his Word and by his Spirit.

We should be fulfilling these commitments in the context of fellowship in a local church, the community of God's people, under the headship of Jesus Christ. We are not meant to do this alone. We need one another. That's why Jesus instituted the church. Finally, at the opening of each new lesson you were required to read specific passages of Scripture and memorize at least one verse from each Scripture selection. That's a total of ten verses memorized. Write them out below:

1)_____
2)_____
3)_____
4)_____
5)_____
6)_____
7)_____

8)_____

9)_____

10)_____

If you review these at least weekly, they will be yours for God's Spirit to use as you live and walk with him daily.

Resolve to:

1. Renew my determination to faithfully carry out the promises I've made to God.
2. Focus on loving God with all my heart, soul, mind, and strength and my neighbor as myself.

_____ (Initial here)

As you fulfill these commitments, making them part of your life, humbly walking with the Lord in the power of his Spirit and putting the Word of God into practice, you will discover your purpose within God's purposes. And you will be living the answer to the question "How should we then live?"

"Oh, the depth of the riches both of the wisdom and knowledge of God! How unsearchable are His judgments and unfathomable His ways! For who has known the mind of the Lord, or who became His counselor? Or who has first given to Him that it might be paid back to him again? For from Him and through Him and to Him are all things. To Him be the glory forever. Amen."
(Romans 11:33–36)

Growth through Crisis Worksheet

God clearly states in his Word that one of his purposes is to conform us, his children, to the image of Jesus Christ. We are to become like him, to take on and reflect his character (Romans 8:29). Jesus and the writers of the New Testament all agree on that point (Matthew 5:48; Romans 5:1–4; James 1:4; 1 Peter 2:21–23; 2 Peter1:3–11). God uses the good and especially the hard times in our lives to shape us.

To "walk in the Spirit" of God is to live putting into practice the character traits of God, of Jesus Christ. The Apostle Paul summarized for us what the results of living in the Spirit are, likening it to fruit, the natural outgrowth of a healthy plant (Galatians 6:22-23).

This worksheet is a tool we can use as we go through a crisis (or reflect on a past crisis) to help us fulfill the purpose of God that we become conformed to the image of Jesus Christ, taking on his character traits.

1. What is/was the crisis?

    _____

2. How am I responding/did I respond? Describe.

    _____
    _____
    _____
    _____

3. To what degree do I think I am manifesting/I manifested these elements of the fruit of the Spirit of God in my response to the crisis? Describe how these are/ were manifested.

    Love

    _____

    Joy

    _____

Peace

_____

Patience

_____

Kindness

_____

Goodness

_____

Faithfulness/Truthfulness

_____

Gentleness

_____

Self-control

_____

4. What is/was my fear or doubt in the midst of the crisis?

_____

5. What is/was my belief about God in the crisis? What Scriptures am I using/did I use while going through the crisis?

_____

6. Am I taking/did I take this crisis to God and am I waiting/did I wait for his response?

_____

7. If God is indeed a Good Father and he has allowed this to happen, what is he teaching/what did he teach me through this?

_____

8. How has/was my character deepened through this crisis?

_____

9. How is God using my circumstances to help others (e.g. contagious love, faith, courage, etc.)? Ask members of your support group to share their observations of how or if God is using your experience to help them or others.

_____

A Last Word

No Bible study is exhaustive. There will always be more to say, more to consider. That is true because of our finiteness and God's infiniteness. "How unsearchable are His judgments and unfathomable His ways!" (Romans 11:33).

It would take more than a lifetime—it will take an eternity—to begin to scratch the surface of the "depth of the riches both of the wisdom and knowledge of God" (Romans 11:33a).

Therefore, with Paul we say, "The goal of our instruction is love from a pure heart and a good conscience and a sincere faith" (1 Timothy 1:5).

This Bible study is simply a means to do what the writer of the book of Hebrews said we should do for one another, "Stimulate one another to love and good deeds" (Hebrews 10:24). The goal of this Bible study is to assist you to produce in yourself the qualities of love, a pure heart, a good conscience, and a sincere faith by pointing you to the Word of God and the God of the Word. What you do with it is up to you.

Jesus put it all into a few words, simple yet profound: "'You shall love the Lord your God with all your heart, and with all your soul, and with all your mind.' This is the great and foremost commandment. 39The second is like it, 'You shall love your neighbor as yourself.' On these two commandments depend the whole Law and the Prophets" (Matthew 22:37–40).

Jesus summed up in these two verses the whole of the Word of God. All of Scripture either illustrates or expounds upon them so that we may learn how to live them. And if we focus on living out these two commandments, we shall indeed be doing the will of God, fulfilling his purposes in the world.

"And now I commend you to God and to the word of his grace, which is able to build you up and to give you the inheritance among all those who are sanctified" (Acts 20:32 ESV).

Let us be about our Father's business!

It is my prayer that this Bible study has been helpful to you. If you have questions for me or want to see what I'm currently writing about, visit my website at https://jacquelinegwallace.com.

Join the community!

Resources for Further Study

Books, blog posts, articles and sermons are all potential sources of continued learning and encouragement from others for our own life journey, written by a broad range of Christians, many going through suffering, who share their own learning and growth experiences.

Listed below are several resources to use. Included are short but powerful blog posts, articles, and books. Our contemporaries wrote some of them while those who have gone before us wrote others, classics of the Christian faith among them. God still speaks through his people.

Christian Living: Growing and Going Deeper with God

Books:

Joseph Bentz, *Nothing is Wasted: How God Redeems What Is Broken*, (Kansas City, MO: Beacon Hill Press, 2016)

Kenneth Boa, *Rewriting Your Broken Story: The Power of an Eternal Perspective*, (Downers Grove, IL: InterVarsity Press, 2016)

Kenneth Boa, *Life in the Presence of God: Practices for Living in Light of Eternity*, (Downers Grove, IL: InterVarsity Press, 2017)

Janet O. Hagberg and Robert A. Guelich, *The Critical Journey*, (Salem, WI: Sheffield Publishing Company, 1989, 1995)

Watchman Nee, *The Normal Christian Life*, (Uhrichsville, OH: Barbour Publishing, Inc.)

Leo Tolstoy, *Where Love is, There God is Also*, (Nashville, TN: Thomas Nelson, Inc., Publishers, 1993)

A.W. Tozer, *The Knowledge of the Holy: The Attributes of God: Their Meaning in the Christian Life*, (New York: HarperCollins)

A.W. Tozer, *How to be Filled with the Holy Spirit*, (Chicago: Moody Publishers, 2016)

Article:

Dr. Chuck Kraft, "Allegiance, Truth and Power: Three crucial dimensions for Christian living," The Pneuma Review, www.pneumareview.com

Blog posts:

Katy Key, "Yes, Lord!" July 7, 2018, *Journey with Katy*, https://journeywithkaty. wordpress.com/2018/07/17/yes-lord/

Rachel Starr Thomson, "The End of Separation: The Deeper Meaning of Faith and Healing," July 24, 2018, *Rachel Starr Thomson-Exploring the Kingdom of God*, http://rachelstarrthomson.com/2018/07/24/the-end-of-separation -the-deeper-meaning-of-faith-and-healing/

The church

Books:

Albert Barnes, Barnes Notes on 1 Corinthians 3, Commentary, http://biblehub.com/ commentaries/barnes/1_corinthians/3.htm

Alan Hirsch and Lance Ford, *Right Here, Right Now: Everyday Mission for Everyday People*, (Grand Rapids: Baker Books, 2011)

Community

Pastor Rick Warren, "Do You Have a Safety Net?" http://pastorrick.com/devotional/ english%2fdo-you-have-a-safety-net1?roi=echo7-32565103814-52490035- 811125b2a2f827643d178d2661886e32&

Forgiveness

Book:

Mclissa Spoclstra, *Joseph: The Journey to Forgiveness* (Nashville: Abingdon Women, 2015)

Blog post:

Debbie W. Wilson, "Forgiveness Brings FREEDOM, Part 1," February 25, 2013, *Refreshing Faith*, https://debbiewwilson.com/forgiveness-brings-freedom-part-1/

God's Correction/Dealing with Self-pity

Blog post:

Rebecca Luella Miller, "To Accept or Not Accept God's Correction," October 30, 2017, *A Christian Worldview of Fiction*, https://rebeccaluellamiller.wordpress.com/2017/10/30/to-accept-or-not-to-accept-gods-correction/

Rachel Starr Thomson, "Beyond 'Lord, Lord': Where Reformations Go Wrong and How We Can Enter the Kingdom," November 14, 2017, *Rachel Starr Thomson-Exploring the Kingdom of God*, https://rachelstarrthomson.com/beyond-lord-lord-reformations-go-wrong-can-enter-kingdom/

God's Purposes

Books:

Os Guinness, *The Call: Finding and Fulfilling the Central Purpose of Your Life*, (Nashville: W Publishing Group a Division of Thomas Nelson, 2003)

Os Guinness, *Rising to the Call: Discover the Ultimate Purpose of Your Life*, (Nashville: Thomas Nelson, 2003)

Collin Hansen and John Woodbridge, *A God-Sized Vision: Revival Stories That Stretch and Stir*, (Grand Rapids: Zondervan, 2010)

Norm Lewis, *Priority One: What God Wants*, (Waynesboro, GA: OM Literature, 1988),

Ralph Winter and Steven C. Hawthorne, eds., *Perspectives on the World Christian Movement: A Reader, Third Edition*, (Pasadena: William Carey Library, 1999)

J. I. Packer, *Knowing God*, (Downers Grove, IL: InterVarsity Press, 1973, 1993)

Rachel Starr Thomson, *"Your Kingdom Calling: 3 Keys to Discovering Your Calling and Purpose in the Kingdom of God."* An ebook available at Amazon and other retailers.

Blog posts:

Dr. Jim Denison, "The Surprising Tour de Force at the Tour de France," July 13, 2018, *Denison Forum: The Daily Article*, https://www.denisonforum.org/columns/daily-article/surprising-tour-de-force-tour-de-france-2/

Dr. Jim Denison, "Pro Football Player Rescues Man Trapped in Car that Plunged Off Parking Garage," July 18, 2018, *Denison Forum: The Daily Article*, https://www.denisonforum.org/?s=pro-football+player

Bill Sweeney, "The Man In the Mirror," August 3, 2017, "About Bill" tab, *Unshakable Hope*, https://unshakablehope.com/2017/08/03/the-man-in-the-mirror/

Bill Sweeney, "Just Imagine," July 2, 2018, *Unshakable Hope*, https://unshakablehope. com/2018/07/02/just-imagine/

Hope

Book:

Craig Groeschel, *Hope in the Dark: Believing God Is Good When Life Is Not*, (Grand Rapids: Zondervan, 2018)

Blog post:

Jim Denison, "Our Hope Is Coming," by guest blogger Steven Longoria, August 17, 2018, *Denison Forum: The Daily Article*, https://mailchi.mp/denisonforum/ our-hope-is-coming?e=7c01b91d86

Living out the teachings of Jesus

Blog posts:

Rachel Starr Thomson, "Building on the Rock: The Law of Christ and the Role of Works in the Christian Life (Part 1)," November 28, 2017, *Rachel Starr Thomson-Exploring the Kingdom of God*, https://rachelstarrthomson.com/ building-rock-law-christ-role-works-christian-life-part-1/

Rachel Starr Thomson, "Building on the Rock: The Law of Christ and the Role of Works in the Christian Life (Part 2)," December 5, 2017, *Rachel Starr Thomson-Exploring the Kingdom of God*, https://rachelstarrthomson.com/ building-rock-law-christ-role-works-christian-life-part-2/

Jim Denison, "Why was Helen Mirren called a 'queen among mortals'?" March 9, 2018, https://mailchi.mp/denisonforum/dailyarticle2018-3-9?e=7c01b91d86

Prayer

Books:

Lynn Donovan, Dineen Miller, SUM Community, *Winning Them With Prayer*, (Temecula, CA: Three Keys Publishing, 2017) This book is about praying for non-Christian spouses.

John Eldredge, *Moving Mountains: Praying with Passion, Confidence and Authority*, (Nashville, TN: Nelson Books, an Imprint of Thomas Nelson, 2016)

Sarah Forgrave, *Prayers for Hope and Healing: Seeking God's Strength As You Face Health Challenges*, (Eugene, OR: Harvest House Publishers, 2017)

John MacArthur, *Alone with God*, (Colorado Springs, CO: David C. Cook, 1981)

Rachel Starr Thomson, *Heart to Heart: Meeting With God in the Lord's Prayer,* (Little Dozen Press, 2012)

Philip Yancey, *Prayer: Does It Make Any Difference?*, (Grand Rapids, MI: Zondervan). I consider this book a "Must Read."

Messages/Sermons:

Pastor Dane Aaker, Centerpoint Church, Colton, CA, sermon, "Prayer 2018," January 7, 2018, Video and Notes:

Sermon video: https://www.youtube.com/watch?v=Z_UUC-bNdQ8&t=45s

Sermon Notes for January 2018: https://static1.squarespace.com/static/57c9f03146c3c44136eae179/t/5a4ff093e4966bf981936c11/1515188374530/01-07-2017.pdf

John Piper, "Ask Whatever You Wish," January 10, 1993, http://www.desiringgod.org/messages/ask-whatever-you-wish

Blog posts:

Rachel Starr Thomson, "'Lead Us Not Into Temptation': The Prayer You Didn't Know God Wanted You to Pray," April 4, 2017, *Rachel Starr Thomson-Exploring the Kingdom of God*, https://rachelstarrthomson.com/lead-us-temptation-prayer-didnt-know-god-wanted-pray/

Rachel Starr Thomson, "Pray Like This: How to Pray the Pattern in the Lord's Prayer," January 31, 2017, *Rachel Starr Thomson-Exploring the Kingdom of God*, https://rachelstarrthomson.com/pray-like-this-how-to-pray-the-pattern-in-the-lords-prayer/

Proving the truth by the Scriptures

Blog posts:

Payte Johnson, "You Can Understand Deeper Theology," paytej.com, February 23, 2018, http://paytej.com/you-can-understand-deeper-theology/

Payte Johnson, "Why Pastors Talk About Greek Words," paytej.com, October 11, 2017, http://paytej.com/why-pastors-talk-about-greek-words/

Payte Johnson, "Feelings Are Important, But Don't Follow Them," paytej.com, March 17, 2018, http://paytej.com/feelings-are-important-dont-follow-them/

Susanne Maynes, "How To Be Certain That What You Believe Is True," March 7, 2017, *Unleashing Your Courageous Compassion*, http://www.susannemaynes.com/certain-believe-true/

Debbie W. Wilson, "12 Traits of Unsafe People," August 28, 2017, *Refreshing Faith*, https://debbiewwilson.com/12-traits-of-unsafe-people/

Suffering

Book:

Steven M. Southwick and Dennis S. Charney, *Resilience: The Science of Mastering Life's Greatest Challenges*, (Cambridge, UK: Cambridge University Press, 2018)

Blog post:

Rachel Starr Thomson, "Hope Is What Allows Me To Be Here": Suffering with Christ in Mosul, Iraq, a guest blog post by Glen Wiffin, September 26, 2017, *Rachel Starr Thomson-Exploring the Kingdom of God*, https://rachelstarrthomson.com/hope-allows-suffering-christ-mosul-iraq/

Your story

Donald Davis, "How the story transforms the teller," You Tube, https://www.youtube.com/results?search_query=How+the+story+transforms+the+teller

Blog posts:

Susanne Maynes, "Five Honest Questions to Test the Depth of Your Faith," August 23, 2017, *Unleashing Your Courageous Compassion*, http://www.susannemaynes.com/5-honest-questions-test-depth-faith/

Debbie W. Wilson, "Why It's Reasonable to Trust God in Your Pain," March 28, 2017, *Refreshing Faith*, https://debbiewwilson.com/why-trust-god-in-pain/

Debbie W. Wilson, "How God Rescued Me from Despair," April 4, 2017, *Refreshing Faith*, https://debbiewwilson.com/god-rescued-despair/

Endnotes

Lesson 5

[1] C.S. Lewis, *The Problem of Pain* (New York: HarperCollins, 2001), pp. 94-95

[2] Oxford University Press. *The Concise Oxford Dictionary*. 10th edition. New York: Oxford University Press, Inc., 1999

Lesson 6

[3] *Hallowed* means "holy or blessed." Merriam-Webster Online Dictionary, copyright © 2015 by Merriam-Webster, Incorporated. All rights reserved. http://www.merriam-webster.com/

Lesson 7

[4] Wm. D. Mounce, *Interlinear for the Rest of Us* (Grand Rapids, MI: Zondervan, 2006), 54

[5] John Ortberg, *Faith and Doubt* (Grand Rapids, MI: Zondervan, 2008), 79

Lesson 8

[6] *Merriam-Webster Dictionary,* s.v. "persist," https://www.merriam-webster.com/dictionary/persist

[7] The "elect" refers to the people of God.

[8] A parable is a story from everyday life that teaches a spiritual truth.

[9] *Brokenness to Beauty*, chapter 9, page 56 and chapter 12, page 78

Lesson 9

10 *Oxford Dictionaries, s.v.* "community," https://en.oxforddictionaries.com/definition/us/community

11 second definition of community from Oxford Dictionaries online

Lesson 10

12 Debbie W. Wilson, "Why It's Reasonable to Trust God in Your Pain," https://debbiewwilson.com/ why-trust-god-in-pain/

13 Oxford Dictionary, s.v. "redemption" means "The action of regaining or gaining possession of something in exchange for payment, or clearing a debt." https://en.oxforddictionaries.com/definition/redemption.
"For you know that you were redeemed from your empty way of life ... not with perishable things like silver or gold, but with the precious blood of Christ" (1 Peter 1:18–19 HCSB). "In him we have redemption through his blood, the forgiveness of sins. ... And you also were included in Christ when you heard the message of truth, the gospel of your salvation. When you believed, you were marked in him with a seal, the promised Holy Spirit, who is a deposit guaranteeing our inheritance until the redemption of those who are God's possession—to the praise of his glory" (Ephesians 1:7, 13–14 NIV). "... waiting eagerly for our adoption as sons, the redemption of our body" (Romans 8:23).

14 Genesis 3:15 Many consider this verse the protevangelium, the first announcement of the gospel. This is the first prophecy about the Messiah (Christ), who through His death on the cross and resurrection would ultimately defeat Satan, the power behind the serpent, with a death blow. See Is 9:6; Matt 1:23; Luke 1:31; Rom 16:20; Gal 4:4; Rev 12:17 (AMP footnote).

About the Author

Jacqueline Wallace is no spectator of life's struggles. Diagnosed at fifteen with Myasthenia Gravis, a severe muscle weakness, the author began learning to live with a life-changing, often life-threatening chronic disease. Forty years later, with a diagnosis of breast cancer, the author brought to bear the basic truths that had guided her ongoing transformation from brokenness to inner beauty and strength, truths learned in the midst of struggles and suffering.

Wallace is a participant with all who suffer, physically and otherwise, and demonstrates through her life and writing the way to a vibrant, joyful, and purposeful life. The truths she lives by are unpacked in her book and companion Bible Study so that she may share them with others.

Jacqueline Wallace lives in southern California with her husband, Randy, and their black cat, Columbia. Her two sons, daughters-in-law, and five grandchildren live nearby.

Visit Jacqueline's website at
www.JacquelineGWallace.com.
Get your free gift when you subscribe.

Printed in the United States
By Bookmasters